<u>Brainteaser</u>

MW01514738

Embark on a thrilling journey of wit and wisdom with 'Brainteasers & Bafflers'! Packed with mind-bending riddles and intriguing facts, this compendium will delight curious minds and puzzle enthusiasts alike. Unleash your inner detective and delve into a world of intellectual challenges, quirky trivia, and endless fun!

- Brainy Kids Press

If you like the book, please review us at Amazon

If you like the book, please review us at Amazon

Category: Science

Question	Answer
Can a snail sleep for three years?	Yes, some snail species can sleep for up to three years.
How many types of cells are in the human body?	There are over 200 different types of cells in the human body.
Can a cockroach survive without its head?	Yes, a cockroach can survive for several weeks without its head.
Is it possible for a human to spontaneously combust?	No, there is no scientific evidence to support spontaneous human combustion.
Can a person sneeze with their eyes open?	No, it is impossible to sneeze with your eyes open.
Can lightning strike the same place twice?	Yes, lightning can strike the same place twice or even multiple times.
Do all animals have brains?	No, some animals like sponges and jellyfish do not have brains.
How long does it take for a fingernail to grow?	It takes about six months for a fingernail to grow from base to tip.
Can a person live without a heart?	No, a human cannot live without a heart.
What is the largest animal on earth?	The blue whale is the largest animal on earth.

Are you Ready for the Challenge- What Am I?

1. I have no body, but I can be heavy; I am often silent but can make a loud sound. I am present in every season, and my form is ever-changing. What am I?

2. I am often bright but never shine, you can create me but not touch me, and I can be still or in motion. What am I?

3. I am present in every home, but I am not a family member. I have a memory but no mind. I can speak, but I have no voice. What am I?

4. Though I am not alive, I can grow, and I can change the way you see the world. What am I?

5. I am made up of letters, but I am not a word. I help you find your way, but I am not a map. What am I?

6. I am a symbol of hope and peace, but I am not a dove. I am a place of rest, but I am not a bed. What am I?

7. What has no beginning, no end, and no middle, but can still hold things together?

8. I am a source of inspiration for many, and I create beauty that lasts for centuries. Yet, I am intangible and cannot be held. What am I?

9. I am never wrong but also never right. I am essential to decision-making but never make decisions myself. What am I?

Category: History

Question	Answer
How many US Presidents have been assassinated?	Four US Presidents have been assassinated: Abraham Lincoln, James A. Garfield, William McKinley, and John F. Kennedy.
Who was the first woman to receive a Nobel Prize?	Marie Curie was the first woman to receive a Nobel Prize.
When was the Great Wall of China built?	The Great Wall of China was built between the 3rd century BC and the 17th century AD.
Who was the first person to circumnavigate the world?	Ferdinand Magellan was the first person to circumnavigate the world.
How many people died in the Holocaust?	An estimated 6 million Jewish people died in the Holocaust.
Who invented the telephone?	Alexander Graham Bell is credited with inventing the telephone.
When did World War II start and end?	World War II started in 1939 and ended in 1945.
Who was the first African American to become president of the United States?	Barack Obama was the first African American to become president of the United States.
Who was the first man to walk on the moon?	Neil Armstrong was the first man to walk on the moon.
What year did the Titanic sink?	The Titanic sank in 1912.

10.   I can make you strong, but too much of me can make you weak. I am both a friend and an enemy. What am I?

11. I'm filled with secrets but reveal no lies. I can transport you to new worlds but never leave your side. What am I?

12.   I can be light as air or heavy as stone, but my fate is tied to the wind. What am I?

13. I am present in every language but never spoken. What am I?

14.   I can be tall or short, thick or thin, and sometimes I disappear. What am I?

15. I keep the time but have no hands. What am I?

16.   I am a silent guide that can show you the world but never leave the room. What am I?

17.   I am always running but never out of breath. What am I?

18.   I can be thin as a thread or wide as a river, but I always move forward. What am I?

Category: Animals

Question	Answer
Can penguins fly?	No, penguins cannot fly.
How long can a giraffe's tongue grow?	A giraffe's tongue can grow up to 18 inches long.
How fast can a cheetah run?	A cheetah can run up to speeds of 70 miles per hour.
Can a kangaroo jump backward?	Yes, kangaroos can jump both forward and backward.
How many legs does a spider have?	Most spiders have eight legs.
What is the smallest mammal in the world?	The bumblebee bat is the smallest mammal in the world.
Can a crocodile stick out its tongue?	No, a crocodile cannot stick out its tongue.
What is the largest bird in the world?	The ostrich is the largest bird in the world.
How long can a sloth sleep for?	Sloths can sleep for up to 20 hours a day
Can an octopus change colors?	Yes, an octopus can change its colors to blend in with its surroundings.

19. I can be found in every corner of the world but can vanish with a simple close. What am I?

20. I bring people together but have no hands to hold them. What am I?

21. I can light up the night without a flame. What am I?

22. I have no voice but can be heard by all. What am I?

23. I am a place of comfort but can be a source of fear. What am I?

24. I can be sweet or bitter, enjoyed by many or just a few. What am I?

25. I am a part of your body but can be shared with others. What am I?

26. I am weightless, but you can see me, and I will disappear if I get wet. What am I?

27. I can be worn or consumed but never held. What am I?

Category: Sports

Question	Answer
What is the oldest sport in the world?	Wrestling is considered the oldest sport in the world.
Who has won the most Olympic gold medals?	Michael Phelps has won the most Olympic gold medals with 23.
How many players are on a soccer team?	There are 11 players on a soccer team.
Who was the first African American to play Major League Baseball?	Jackie Robinson was the first African American to play Major League Baseball.
What is the highest score you can get in bowling?	The highest score you can get in bowling is 300.
How many holes are on a standard golf course?	There are 18 holes on a standard golf course.
Who has won the most Grand Slam titles in tennis?	Roger Federer has won the most Grand Slam titles in tennis with 20.
What is the fastest pitch ever thrown in baseball?	The fastest pitch ever thrown in baseball was 105.1 miles per hour.
What is the most popular sport in the world?	Soccer is the most popular sport in the world.
Who is considered the greatest basketball player of all time?	Michael Jordan is considered the greatest basketball player of all time.

28. I am a key that can open no lock but can unlock your imagination. What am I?

29. I can be created by the sun or by humans, but I can't be touched or held. What am I?

30. I am a friend to the traveler but never leave my post. What am I?

31. I am found in the darkest corners, but I fear the light. What am I?

32. I have many layers but no skin. What am I?

33. I can be a friend or a foe, but I never choose sides. What am I?

34. I have many faces but only show one at a time. What am I?

35. I can be a melody or a cacophony, but I'm created by hands. What am I?

36. I can be a source of joy or a cause for tears, but I never express emotion. What am I?

Category: Art and Entertainment

Question	Answer
Who painted the Mona Lisa?	Leonardo da Vinci painted the Mona Lisa.
What is the highest-grossing movie of all time?	Avatar is the highest-grossing movie of all time.
Who wrote the Harry Potter book series?	J.K. Rowling wrote the Harry Potter book series.
What is the name of the world's largest art museum?	The Louvre is the world's largest art museum.
Who is the best-selling music artist of all time?	The Beatles are the best-selling music artist of all time.
What is the most-watched television show of all time?	The Super Bowl is the most-watched television show of all time.
Who created the sculpture of David?	Michelangelo created the sculpture of David.
What is the name of the world's oldest opera house?	The Teatro di San Carlo is the world's oldest opera house.
Who directed the Star Wars movies?	George Lucas directed the Star Wars movies.
Who painted The Starry Night?	Vincent van Gogh painted The Starry Night.

37.　I can be broken but never fixed. What am I?

38.　I have many keys, but I can't open any doors. What am I?

39.　I can be a single note or an entire symphony, but I can't be played. What am I?

40.　I can be found in every season, but I don't change with the weather. What am I?

41.　I can be captured but never controlled. What am I?

42.　I can create a smile, but I can't be seen. What am I?

43.　I can make you stumble, but I never move. What am I?

44.　I am often followed but never chased. What am I?

45.　I can be consumed but never eaten. What am I?

Category: Technology

Question	Answer
What was the first video game ever created?	Pong was the first video game ever created.
Who invented the World Wide Web?	Tim Berners-Lee invented the World Wide Web.
What is the most popular social media platform?	Facebook is the most popular social media platform.
What is the name of the first computer ever made?	The first computer ever made was called the Electronic Numerical Integrator and Computer (ENIAC).
Who invented the telephone?	Alexander Graham Bell is credited with inventing the telephone.
What is the name of the world's first smartphone?	The IBM Simon was the world's first smartphone.
Who created the first computer mouse?	Douglas Engelbart created the first computer mouse.
What is the most popular search engine?	Google is the most popular search engine.
What is the name of the world's first computer virus?	The first computer virus was called the Creeper virus
Who invented the modern light bulb?	Thomas Edison is credited with inventing the modern light bulb.

46. I can be opened but never closed. What am I?

47. I can be seen at night but never during the day. What am I?

48. I can be a source of warmth and light but can also cause destruction. What am I?

49. I can be shared with many but owned by none. What am I?

50. I can be as big as a mountain or as small as a grain of sand, but I never weigh anything. What am I?

51. I can be full of life but never breathe. What am I?

52. I can bind things together but have no hands. What am I?

53. I can be everywhere at once but only seen by few. What am I?

54. I am a feast for the eyes, but I cannot be eaten. What am I?

Category: Geography

Question	Answer
What is the capital of Brazil?	Brasilia is the capital of Brazil.
What is the tallest mountain in the world?	Mount Everest is the tallest mountain in the world.
What is the longest river in the world?	The Nile River is the longest river in the world.
What is the smallest country in the world?	Vatican City is the smallest country in the world.
What is the largest country in the world by land area?	Russia is the largest country in the world by land area.
What is the highest waterfall in the world?	Angel Falls is the highest waterfall in the world.
What is the largest desert in the world?	The Sahara Desert is the largest desert in the world.
What is the only continent that is also a country?	Australia is the only continent that is also a country.
What is the capital of Canada?	Ottawa is the capital of Canada.
What is the southernmost continent in the world?	Antarctica is the southernmost continent in the world.

55.   I can be vibrant and colorful, but I have no pigments. What am I?

56.   I can be a source of pride or a symbol of disgrace, but I am not an emotion. What am I?

57.   I can be a welcome surprise or an unwelcome intruder, but I cannot be controlled. What am I?

58.   I can be a cover or a barrier, but I am not a shield. What am I?

59.   I can be strong and flexible, but I am not a muscle. What am I?

60.   I can be held in one hand but fill an entire room. What am I?

61.   I can be stretched or compressed, but I have no physical form. What am I?

62.   I can be as vast as the ocean or as small as a pond, but I am not a body of water. What am I?

63.   I can be created or destroyed, but I can never be touched. What am I?

Category: Food and Drink

Question	Answer
What is the most popular fruit in the world?	Mangoes are the most popular fruit in the world.
What is the national dish of Italy?	Pizza is considered the national dish of Italy.
What is the most consumed beverage in the world?	Water is the most consumed beverage in the world.
What is the hottest chili pepper in the world?	The Carolina Reaper is currently the hottest chili pepper in the world.
What is the most expensive spice in the world?	Saffron is the most expensive spice in the world.
What is the national dish of Spain?	Paella is considered the national dish of Spain.
What is the most popular fast food chain in the world?	McDonald's is the most popular fast food chain in the world.
What is the national dish of Thailand?	Pad Thai is considered the national dish of Thailand.
What is the most expensive coffee in the world?	Kopi Luwak is the most expensive coffee in the world.
What is the national dish of Mexico?	Tacos are considered the national dish of Mexico.

64. I can be measured but never seen. What am I?

65. I can be a path or a barrier, but I am not a road. What am I?

66. I can be a sign of wealth or a symbol of poverty, but I am not money. What am I?

67. I can be a source of comfort or a cause of distress, but I am not a person. What am I?

68. I can be a reflection or an illusion, but I have no substance. What am I?

69. I can be a window to the world or a door to another realm. What am I?

70. I can be the essence of life or a symbol of death, but I am not a living being. What am I?

71. I can be a source of knowledge or a means of escape, but I am not a teacher. What am I?

72. I can be a symbol of power or a sign of weakness, but I am not a ruler. What am I?

Category: Health and Medicine

Question	Answer
What is the largest organ in the human body?	The skin is the largest organ in the human body.
What is the name of the smallest bone in the human body?	The stapes bone in the ear is the smallest bone in the human body.
What is the most common blood type in the world?	O positive is the most common blood type in the world.
How many bones are in the human body?	There are 206 bones in the human body.
What is the name of the hormone that regulates sleep?	Melatonin is the hormone that regulates sleep.
What is the name of the organ that produces insulin?	The pancreas is the organ that produces insulin.
What is the most common mental illness in the world?	Depression is the most common mental illness in the world.
What is the name of the virus that causes AIDS?	The human immunodeficiency virus (HIV) causes AIDS.
What is the name of the largest artery in the human body?	The aorta is the largest artery in the human body.
What is the name of the protein that gives skin its color?	Melanin is the protein that gives skin its color.

73.   I can be a cause of celebration or a source of dread, but I am not an event. What am I?

74.   I can be a beacon of hope or a harbinger of doom, but I am not a messenger. What am I?

75.   I can be a friend to the lonely or a companion to the busy, but I am not a pet. What am I?

76.   I can be a source of inspiration or a subject of frustration, but I am not an emotion. What am I?

77.   I can be a treasured keepsake or a discarded trinket, but I am not a possession. What am I?

78.   I can be a challenge to the strong or a comfort to the weak, but I am not a test. What am I?

79.   I can be a symbol of love or a sign of betrayal, but I am not a feeling. What am I?

80.   I can be a source of life or a cause of decay, but I am not a force of nature. What am I?

81.   I can be a source of calm or a catalyst for chaos, but I am not a person. What am I?

Category: Mythology and Folklore

Question	Answer
What is the name of the Greek god of the sky and thunder?	Zeus is the Greek god of the sky and thunder.
What is the name of the Norse god of thunder?	Thor is the Norse god of thunder.
What is the name of the Roman goddess of love?	Venus is the Roman goddess of love.
What is the name of the Greek goddess of wisdom?	Athena is the Greek goddess of wisdom.
What is the name of the Greek god of wine?	Dionysus is the Greek god of wine.
What is the name of the Norse god of mischief?	Loki is the Norse god of mischief.
What is the name of the Greek god of the sea?	Poseidon is the Greek god of the sea.
What is the name of the Greek goddess of the hunt?	Artemis is the Greek goddess of the hunt.
What is the name of the Greek god of war?	Ares is the Greek god of war.
What is the name of the Roman god of love?	Cupid is the Roman god of love.

82. I can be a cherished memory or a painful reminder, but I am not an experience. What am I?

83. I can be a means of communication or a source of isolation, but I am not a language. What am I?

84. I can be a path to the stars or a route to the depths, but I am not a vehicle. What am I?

85. I can be a symbol of freedom or a sign of captivity, but I am not a flag. What am I?

86. I can be a source of nourishment or a cause of illness, but I am not a food. What am I?

87. I can be a guide to the lost or a comfort to the weary, but I am not a compass. What am I?

88. I can be a fleeting moment or an eternal presence, but I am not a ghost. What am I?

89. I can be a ray of sunshine or a shroud of darkness, but I am not a weather phenomenon. What am I?

90. I can be a treasure trove of wisdom or a repository of nonsense, but I am not a library. What am I?

Category: Miscellaneous

Question	Answer
What is the name of the instrument used to measure earthquakes?	A seismograph is the instrument used to measure earthquakes.
What is the name of the smallest country in Africa?	Seychelles is the smallest country in Africa.
What is the name of the oldest university in the world?	The University of Bologna is the oldest university in the world.
What is the name of the instrument used to measure wind speed?	Anemometers are the instruments used to measure wind speed.
What is the name of the smallest ocean in the world?	The Arctic Ocean is the smallest ocean in the world.
What is the name of the device used to measure blood pressure?	Sphygmomanometers are the devices used to measure blood pressure.
What is the name of the tallest building in the world?	The Burj Khalifa is the tallest building in the world.
What is the name of the device used to measure time?	Chronometers are the devices used to measure time
What is the name of the metal that is liquid at room temperature?	Mercury is the metal that is liquid at room temperature
What is the name of the instrument used to measure humidity?	Hygrometers are the instruments used to measure humidity

91. I can be a barrier to progress or a catalyst for change, but I am not a wall. What am I?

92. I can be a source of warmth or a chilling presence, but I am not a fire. What am I?

93. I can be a vessel for dreams or a container for memories, but I am not a box. What am I?

94. I can be a source of life or a harbinger of death, but I am not a god. What am I?

95. I can be a sign of hope or a symbol of despair, but I am not an omen. What am I?

96. I can be a catalyst for growth or a cause of stagnation, but I am not a nutrient. What am I?

97. I can be a means of expression or a source of oppression, but I am not a voice. What am I?

98. I can be a comforting presence or a source of terror, but I am not a person. What am I?

99. I can be a path to enlightenment or a route to destruction, but I am not a road. What am I?

Category: Science

Question	Answer
Can a human sneeze faster than a cheetah can run?	No, a cheetah can run up to speeds of 70 miles per hour while a human sneeze only reaches up to 100 miles per hour.
How many different smells can a human nose detect?	A human nose can detect over one trillion different smells.
Can a person survive without a certain percentage of their brain?	Yes, a person can survive without up to 50% of their brain.
Is it true that bananas are berries while strawberries are not?	Yes, bananas are berries, while strawberries are not.
Can a person live without their appendix?	Yes, a person can live without their appendix, and it does not have any essential functions in the body.
Is it true that a person's fingerprint remains the same throughout their lifetime?	Yes, a person's fingerprint remains the same throughout their lifetime, and no two people have the same fingerprints.
Can a person's eyes pop out of their sockets if they sneeze too hard?	No, a person's eyes cannot pop out of their sockets if they sneeze too hard.
How many taste buds does an average human have on their tongue?	An average human has about 10,000 taste buds on their tongue.
Can an ostrich's eyes be bigger than its brain?	Yes, an ostrich's eyes are larger than its brain.
Is it possible for a person to have an extra rib?	Yes, it is possible for a person to have an extra rib, and some people are born with this condition called cervical rib.

100. I can be a source of joy or a well of sorrow, but I am not a feeling. What am I?

101. I can be a unifier or a divider, but I am not a ruler. What am I?

102. I can be a spark of life or a harbinger of darkness, but I am not a flame. What am I?

103. I can be a force of nature or a man-made marvel, but I am not a creation. What am I?

104. I can be a guardian of secrets or a revealer of truths, but I am not a detective. What am I?

105. I can be a means of escape or a path to captivity, but I am not a door. What am I?

106. I can be a symbol of peace or a harbinger of war, but I am not a flag. What am I?

107. I can be a source of strength or a cause of weakness, but I am not a muscle. What am I?

108. I can be a fortress of solitude or a hive of activity, but I am not a building. What am I?

Category: History

Question	Answer
Did ancient Egyptians have pet cats?	Yes, ancient Egyptians kept cats as pets and considered them sacred animals.
Who invented the first camera?	The first camera was invented by Joseph Nicéphore Niépce in 1826.
Is it true that the Roman Empire was built on cheese?	No, the Roman Empire was not built on cheese, but it was a staple food in their diet.
Did Vikings wear horned helmets?	No, Vikings did not wear horned helmets, but this myth was popularized in the 19th century.
Who invented the printing press?	Johannes Gutenberg invented the printing press in 1440.
Did ancient Greeks invent democracy?	Yes, ancient Greeks are credited with inventing democracy in the 5th century BC.
Is it true that Julius Caesar was afraid of cats?	No, there is no evidence to support the myth that Julius Caesar was afraid of cats.
Who built the first pyramids in Egypt?	The first pyramids in Egypt were built by the pharaoh Djoser in the 27th century BC.
Is it true that Napoleon was short?	No, Napoleon was actually above average height for his time, and the myth of him being short was a result of propaganda.
Who wrote the novel "To Kill a Mockingbird"?	Harper Lee wrote the novel "To Kill a Mockingbird" in 1960.

109. I can be a beacon of light or a harbinger of shadows, but I am not a lamp. What am I?

110. I can be a source of inspiration or a cause of frustration, but I am not a muse. What am I?

111. I can be sharp, blunt, or curved, but I am not a knife. What am I?

112. I can be a source of joy or a trigger for allergies, but I am not a pet. What am I?

113. I can be as smooth as glass or as rough as sandpaper, but I am not a surface. What am I?

114. I can be a means of connection or a source of separation, but I am not a bridge. What am I?

115. I can be a sign of life or a symbol of loss, but I am not a heartbeat. What am I?

116. I can be as hard as a rock or as soft as a cloud, but I am not a substance. What am I?

117. I can be a messenger of love or a harbinger of heartbreak, but I am not a person. What am I?

Category: Animals

Question	Answer
Can a kangaroo fart?	Yes, kangaroos can fart, and their farts are so powerful that they can knock out predators.
How many hearts does an octopus have?	An octopus has three hearts.
Is it true that sloths only move once a week?	No, this is a common misconception. While sloths are slow-moving animals, they do move more often than once a week.
Do penguins have knees?	Yes, penguins do have knees, but they are located inside their bodies and not visible from the outside.
Is it true that a group of flamingos is called a flamboyance?	Yes, a group of flamingos is called a flamboyance.
Can a hippopotamus swim?	Yes, hippopotamuses are excellent swimmers and can hold their breath for up to five minutes underwater.
Is it true that elephants never forget?	While elephants do have excellent memory, the idea that they never forget is a myth.
Can a chameleon change its color to blend in with any background?	No, chameleons can only change their color to blend in with their immediate surroundings, not any background.
Is it true that a group of owls is called a parliament?	Yes, a group of owls is called a parliament.
Can a giraffe clean its ears with its tongue?	Yes, a giraffe can clean its ears with its tongue, which is more than 18 inches long.
Is it true that a group of crows is called a murder?	Yes, a group of crows is called a murder.

118. I can be a keeper of secrets or a revealer of hidden truths, but I am not a diary. What am I?

119. I can be a means of travel or a source of stability, but I am not a vehicle. What am I?

120. I can be a sign of hope or a reminder of despair, but I am not a rainbow. What am I?

121. I can be a guide for the blind or a tool for the sighted, but I am not a dog. What am I?

122. I can be a source of illumination or a cause of darkness, but I am not a light bulb. What am I?

123. I can be a symbol of unity or a representation of division, but I am not a flag. What am I?

124. I can be a force of nature or a result of human effort, but I am not a storm. What am I?

125. I can be a source of delight or a cause of irritation, but I am not a sensation. What am I?

126. I can be a catalyst for change or a reason for stagnation, but I am not an event. What am I?

Category: Technology

Question	Answer
Is it possible to charge a phone with a potato?	*Yes, it is possible to charge a phone with a potato using a copper wire and a zinc-coated nail.*
Can a robot have emotions?	*No, robots cannot have emotions, but they can be programmed to simulate emotions.*
Is it true that the first computer mouse was made of wood?	*Yes, the first computer mouse was made of wood by Douglas Engelbart in 1963.*
Can a computer get a virus from a USB drive?	*Yes, a computer can get a virus from a USB drive if the drive is infected.*
Is it true that the first website in the world is still online?	*Yes, the first website in the world is still online, and it was created by Tim Berners-Lee in 1991.*
Can a drone deliver a pizza?	*Yes, drones can be used to deliver pizzas, and some companies are already experimenting with this technology.*
Is it true that the first smartphone was made by IBM?	*No, the first smartphone was made by IBM, but by IBM Simon in 1993.*
Can a computer think like a human?	*No, computers cannot think like humans, but they can perform tasks that require intelligence.*
Is it true that Bill Gates once released mosquitoes during a TED talk?	*Yes, Bill Gates released mosquitoes during a TED talk to raise awareness about malaria.*
Can a self-driving car navigate without GPS?	*Yes, self-driving cars can navigate without GPS using sensors and other technologies.*

127. I can be a window into the past or a glimpse into the future, but I am not a time machine. What am I?

128. I can be a link to the world or a barrier to connection, but I am not a chain. What am I?

129. I can be a spark of inspiration or a catalyst for destruction, but I am not a fire. What am I?

130. I can be a comfort to the sad or a cause of laughter, but I am not a person. What am I?

131. I can be a symbol of strength or a sign of fragility, but I am not an object. What am I?

132. I can be a path to safety or a route to danger, but I am not a road. What am I?

133. I can be a source of energy or a cause of exhaustion, but I am not a food. What am I?

134. I can be a force for growth or a reason for decline, but I am not a plant. What am I?

135. I can be a tool for creation or a weapon for destruction, but I am not a machine. What am I?

Category: Sports

Question	Answer
Can a table tennis ball travel faster than a baseball?	Yes, a table tennis ball can travel faster than a baseball, with the fastest recorded speed being over 100 miles per hour.
Is it true that basketball was invented by a Canadian?	No, basketball was invented by James Naismith, an American physical education instructor.
Can a person run a marathon in under two hours?	Yes, a person can run a marathon in under two hours, and the current world record is 1:39:40 set by Eliud Kipchoge.
Is it true that the Olympic Games were originally held for artistic competitions?	Yes, the Olympic Games were originally held for artistic competitions in addition to athletic events.
Can a person swim faster than a crocodile?	Yes, a person can swim faster than a crocodile, but it is not recommended to swim in waters where crocodiles are present.
Is it true that chess is considered a sport?	Yes, chess is recognized as a sport by the International Olympic Committee.
Can a person play professional sports without a college degree?	Yes, a person can play professional sports without a college degree, but some leagues require a minimum age or a certain level of experience.
Is it true that the Wimbledon tennis tournament serves strawberries and cream to its guests?	Yes, strawberries and cream is a traditional dish served at the Wimbledon tennis tournament.
Can a person bowl a perfect game of 300?	Yes, a person can bowl a perfect game of 300 by bowling 12 strikes in a row
Is it true that the Super Bowl is the most-watched television event in the United States?	Yes, the Super Bowl is the most-watched television event in the United States, with millions of viewers tuning in each year.

136. I can be a symbol of hope or a reminder of pain, but I am not a scar. What am I?

137. I can be a guardian of treasures or a keeper of secrets, but I am not a dragon. What am I?

138. I can be a source of solace or a cause of distress, but I am not a pillow. What am I?

139. I can be a measure of time or a reminder of the past, but I am not a clock. What am I?

140. I can be a source of inspiration or a reason for procrastination, but I am not a muse. What am I?

141. I can be a symbol of freedom or a sign of confinement, but I am not a bird. What am I?

142. I can be a key to new worlds or a trap in the familiar, but I am not a door. What am I?

143. I can be a harbinger of life or a bringer of decay, but I am not a plant. What am I?

144. I can be a sign of strength or a mark of vulnerability, but I am not a shield. What am I?

Category: Geography

Question	Answer
Is it true that Canada has more lakes than the rest of the world combined?	Yes, Canada has more lakes than the rest of the world combined, with over three million lakes.
Can a person visit Antarctica as a tourist?	Yes, a person can visit Antarctica as a tourist, but it is highly regulated, and only a limited number of visitors are allowed each year.
Is it true that the Great Barrier Reef is the largest living structure on Earth?	Yes, the Great Barrier Reef is the largest living structure on Earth, and it can be seen from space.
Can a person cross the Sahara Desert by foot?	Yes, a person can cross the Sahara Desert by foot, but it is a dangerous and challenging journey.
Is it true that the Dead Sea is so salty that people can float on its surface?	Yes, the Dead Sea is so salty that people can easily float on its surface due to the high salt content.
Can a person climb Mount Everest without oxygen?	Yes, a person can climb Mount Everest without oxygen, but it is very difficult, and only a few climbers have ever done it.
Is it true that the Amazon Rainforest produces over 20% of the world's oxygen?	Yes, the Amazon Rainforest produces over 20% of the world's oxygen, and it is often referred to as the "lungs of the Earth."
Can a person drive from North America to South America?	Yes, a person can drive from North America to South America using the Pan-American Highway, but it requires crossing several borders and can take months to complete.
Is it true that the Nile River is the longest river in the world?	Yes, the Nile River is the longest river in the world, stretching over 4,000 miles.
Can a person visit all seven continents in one day?	No, it is not possible to visit all seven continents in one day as they are spread across different time zones.

145. I can be a reason for celebration or a cause of disappointment, but I am not a gift. What am I?

146. I can be a source of warmth or a chilling breeze, but I am not a blanket. What am I?

147. I can be a symbol of love or a representation of loss, but I am not a heart. What am I?

148. I can be a force of attraction or a source of repulsion, but I am not a magnet. What am I?

149. I can be a reminder of achievements or a sign of failure, but I am not a trophy. What am I?

150. I can be a source of growth or a cause of destruction, but I am not water. What am I?

151. I can be a pathway to knowledge or a route to confusion, but I am not a book. What am I?

152. I can be a means of relaxation or a source of anxiety, but I am not a vacation. What am I?

153. I can be a mark of progress or a sign of stagnation, but I am not a milestone. What am I?

Category: Art

Question	Answer
Is it true that the Mona Lisa has no eyebrows?	Yes, the Mona Lisa has no eyebrows, and it is believed that it was the fashion during the Renaissance period to shave them.
Can a person be a successful artist without any formal training?	Yes, a person can be a successful artist without any formal training, but it requires talent, dedication, and hard work.
Is it true that the Statue of Liberty was a gift from France to the United States?	Yes, the Statue of Liberty was a gift from France to the United States as a symbol of friendship between the two countries.
Can a person make art with food?	Yes, a person can make art with food, and it is a popular form of art known as food art or culinary art.
Is it true that Vincent van Gogh only sold one painting during his lifetime?	Yes, Vincent van Gogh only sold one painting during his lifetime, but his work is now highly valued and admired.
Can a person use technology to create art?	Yes, a person can use technology to create art, and it has given rise to new forms of digital art such as video art, net art, and interactive art.
Is it true that Michelangelo painted the ceiling of the Sistine Chapel lying on his back?	Yes, Michelangelo painted the ceiling of the Sistine Chapel lying on his back, and it took him four years to complete the work.
Can a person create art using everyday objects?	Yes, a person can create art using everyday objects, and it is a form of art known as found object art or ready-made art.
Is it true that Banksy's identity is unknown?	Yes, Banksy's identity is unknown, and he is a mysterious and elusive street artist known for his political and social commentary.
Can a person create art without using a brush?	Yes, a person can create art without using a brush, and it is a form of art known as non-brush painting, which includes techniques such as finger painting, pouring, and spraying.

154. I can be a source of stability or a cause of chaos, but I am not an anchor. What am I?

155. I can be a tool for expression or a weapon for manipulation, but I am not a pen. What am I?

156. I can be a source of clarity or a cause of confusion, but I am not a lens. What am I?

157. I can be a sign of hope or a symbol of despair, but I am not a message. What am I?

158. I can be a force of unity or a reason for division, but I am not a leader. What am I?

159. I can be a gateway to the unknown or a link to the familiar, but I am not a portal. What am I?

160. I can be a source of life or a harbinger of doom, but I am not a comet. What am I?

161. I can be a mark of wealth or a sign of poverty, but I am not money. What am I?

162. I can be a catalyst for creation or a force of destruction, but I am not an artist. What am I?

Category: Music

Is it true that Beethoven continued to compose music even after he became deaf?	Yes, Beethoven continued to compose music even after he became deaf, and some of his most famous works were created during this time.
Can a person play an instrument without any formal training?	Yes, a person can play an instrument without any formal training, but it requires practice, patience, and dedication.
Is it true that Mozart composed his first piece of music at the age of five?	Yes, Mozart composed his first piece of music at the age of five, and he was a musical prodigy who created many masterpieces during his short life.
Can a person create music using technology?	Yes, a person can create music using technology, and it has given rise to new forms of music such as electronic music, techno, and ambient music.
Is it true that the Beatles performed their last concert on a rooftop?	Yes, the Beatles performed their last concert on a rooftop of their record label's building in London, and it was a surprise performance that drew a large crowd.
Can a person sing without any vocal training?	Yes, a person can sing without any vocal training, but it requires natural talent and an ear for music.
Is it true that Elvis Presley was once told that he couldn't sing?	Yes, Elvis Presley was once told that he couldn't sing and should stick to driving trucks, but he went on to become one of the most successful musicians of all time.
Can a person create music without using instruments?	Yes, a person can create music without using instruments, and it is a form of music known as acapella, which involves using the voice to produce different sounds and melodies.
Is it true that Queen's "Bohemian Rhapsody" was initially criticized by music executives?	Yes, Queen's "Bohemian Rhapsody" was initially criticized by music executives who thought it was too long and too unconventional, but it went on to become one of the most popular and iconic songs of all time.
Can a person compose music without knowing how to read sheet music?	Yes, a person can compose music without knowing how to read sheet music, but it requires a good ear for music and an understanding of basic musical principles.

163. I can be a reason for joy or a cause of sorrow, but I am not an emotion. What am I?

164. I can be a symbol of power or a sign of weakness, but I am not a throne. What am I?

165. I can be a tool for discovery or a means of concealment, but I am not a telescope. What am I?

166. I can be a source of comfort or a cause of unease, but I am not a bed. What am I?

167. I can be a sign of promise or a mark of disappointment, but I am not a contract. What am I?

168. I can be a pathway to adventure or a source of danger, but I am not a trail. What am I?

169. I can be a tool for communication or a cause of misunderstanding, but I am not a language. What am I?

170. I can be a symbol of beauty or a sign of decay, but I am not a flower. What am I?

171. I can be a reason for excitement or a cause of dread, but I am not an event. What am I?

Category: Literature

Question	Answer
Is it true that J.K. Rowling was rejected by several publishers before Harry Potter was finally published?	Yes, J.K. Rowling was rejected by several publishers before Harry Potter was finally published, but it went on to become one of the best-selling book series of all time.
Can a person write a book without any formal training?	Yes, a person can write a book without any formal training, but it requires discipline, creativity, and a love for storytelling.
Is it true that "1984" by George Orwell is a dystopian novel?	Yes, "1984" by George Orwell is a dystopian novel that depicts a totalitarian society in which citizens are oppressed and surveilled by the government.
Can a person write a book using a typewriter?	Yes, a person can write a book using a typewriter, and it was a popular tool for writers before the advent of computers.
Is it true that Jane Austen wrote anonymously during her lifetime?	Yes, Jane Austen wrote anonymously during her lifetime, and it was only after her death that her true identity was revealed.
Can a person write a book using a pen and paper?	Yes, a person can write a book using a pen and paper, and it is a preferred method for some writers who find it more conducive to creativity.
Is it true that "The Great Gatsby" by F. Scott Fitzgerald was a commercial failure during his lifetime?	Yes, "The Great Gatsby" by F. Scott Fitzgerald was a commercial failure during his lifetime, but it is now considered a literary masterpiece and one of the greatest American novels.
Can a person write a book in a different language than their native language?	Yes, a person can write a book in a different language than their native language, but it requires fluency and a good understanding of the grammar and vocabulary of the language.
Is it true that Charles Dickens wrote his novels in installments for magazines?	Yes, Charles Dickens wrote his novels in installments for magazines, and they were published chapter by chapter over a period of months.
Can a person write a book in different genres?	Yes, a person can write a book in different genres, and it allows for more creativity and experimentation in storytelling.

172. I can be a force for protection or a source of vulnerability, but I am not a lock. What am I?

173. I can be a symbol of wisdom or a mark of ignorance, but I am not a book. What am I?

174. I can be a source of inspiration or a cause of disillusionment, but I am not a dream. What am I?

175. I can be a beacon of hope or a harbinger of despair, but I am not a light. What am I?

176. I can be a means of expression or a cause of frustration, but I am not an instrument. What am I?

177. I can be a sign of growth or a symbol of stagnation, but I am not a plant. What am I?

178. I can be a source of motivation or a reason for procrastination, but I am not a goal. What am I?

179. I can be a pathway to the unknown or a link to the familiar, but I am not a path. What am I?

180. I can be a symbol of endurance or a mark of fragility, but I am not a monument. What am I?

Category: Food

Question	Answer
Is it true that chocolate can be addictive?	Yes, chocolate contains a chemical called phenylethylamine that can stimulate the production of endorphins and dopamine in the brain, making it potentially addictive.
Can a person eat healthy while still enjoying fast food?	Yes, a person can eat healthy while still enjoying fast food by making smart choices such as choosing grilled or baked options, avoiding fried foods, and selecting smaller portions
Is it true that some foods can boost your metabolism?	Yes, some foods such as green tea, spicy foods, and protein can boost your metabolism and help you burn more calories.
Can a person be a good cook without any formal training?	Yes, a person can be a good cook without any formal training, but it requires practice, experimentation, and a love for cooking.
Is it true that sushi is traditionally eaten with hands?	Yes, sushi is traditionally eaten with hands, but it is also acceptable to use chopsticks if preferred.
Can a person cook a meal using only a microwave?	Yes, a person can cook a meal using only a microwave, and it is a convenient option for those with limited time or resources.
Is it true that spicy foods can make you feel cooler in hot weather?	Yes, spicy foods can make you feel cooler in hot weather by causing your body to sweat, which can help regulate your body temperature.
Can a person eat a balanced diet without consuming any animal products?	Yes, a person can eat a balanced diet without consuming any animal products by choosing a variety of plant-based foods that provide all the necessary nutrients.
Is it true that bananas are berries?	Yes, bananas are considered berries because they are a fleshy fruit that develops from a single ovary.
Can a person cook a meal without using any salt?	Yes, a person can cook a meal without using any salt, and there are many other spices and herbs that can be used to add flavor.
Is it true that the world's largest pizza was over 13,000 square feet?	Yes, the world's largest pizza was over 13,000 square feet and was made in Italy in 2012.

Are you Ready for the Challenge- What Am I?

181. I can be a force of nature or a product of human creation, but I am not a weather phenomenon. What am I?

182. I can be a means of support or a source of obstruction, but I am not a pillar. What am I?

183. I can be a reason for celebration or a cause of sadness, but I am not a holiday. What am I?

184. I can be a tool for connection or a cause of disconnection, but I am not a bridge. What am I?

185. I can be a symbol of hope or a sign of despair, but I am not a flag. What am I?

186. I can be a force for change or a source of resistance, but I am not a revolution. What am I?

187. I can be a reason for delight or a cause of annoyance, but I am not a sound. What am I?

188. I can be a catalyst for growth or a force of decay, but I am not a fertilizer. What am I?

189. I can be a source of illumination or a cause of obscurity, but I am not a lamp. What am I?

Category: Science

Question	Answer
Is it true that the universe is expanding?	Yes, the universe is expanding, and this was first discovered by astronomer Edwin Hubble in the 1920s.
Can a person see atoms with the naked eye?	No, atoms are too small to be seen with the naked eye and require specialized equipment such as microscopes to be observed.
Is it true that light can travel around the Earth seven and a half times in one second?	Yes, light can travel around the Earth seven and a half times in one second, and it is the fastest known thing in the universe.
Can a person make a battery out of a lemon?	Yes, a person can make a battery out of a lemon by using it as an electrolyte to create a chemical reaction that generates electricity.
Is it true that the Earth's magnetic field protects us from solar winds?	Yes, the Earth's magnetic field protects us from solar winds, which are streams of charged particles that can be harmful to living organisms.
Can a person create a tornado in a bottle?	Yes, a person can create a tornado in a bottle by filling a bottle with water and swirling it to create a vortex.
Is it true that lightning can strike the same place twice?	Yes, lightning can strike the same place twice, and it is more likely to strike tall structures such as buildings and trees.
Can a person create a rainbow using a prism?	Yes, a person can create a rainbow using a prism by refracting white light into its different colors.
Is it true that the sun is a star?	Yes, the sun is a star, and it is the closest star to Earth.
Can a person create a lava lamp at home?	Yes, a person can create a lava lamp at home by using a clear container, water, oil, food coloring, and Alka-Seltzer tablets.

190. I can be a symbol of strength or a sign of weakness, but I am not a fortress. What am I?

191. I can be a means of escape or a source of confinement, but I am not a prison. What am I?

192. I can be a force for healing or a cause of harm, but I am not medicine. What am I?

193. I can be a reason for joy or a source of despair, but I am not an achievement. What am I?

194. I can be a tool for creation or a weapon for destruction, but I am not a factory. What am I?

195. I can be a symbol of unity or a sign of division, but I am not a boundary. What am I?

196. I can be a source of warmth or a cause of shivering, but I am not a fire. What am I?

197. I can be a sign of life or a reminder of mortality, but I am not a heartbeat. What am I?

198. I can be a means of exploration or a source of danger, but I am not a map. What am I?

Category: History

Question	Answer
Is it true that the Great Wall of China is visible from space?	No, the Great Wall of China is not visible from space with the naked eye, but it can be seen in some satellite images.
Can a person visit ancient ruins of civilizations that no longer exist?	Yes, a person can visit ancient ruins of civilizations that no longer exist, and it provides a glimpse into the past and the way of life of ancient peoples.
Is it true that the Titanic sank on its maiden voyage?	Yes, the Titanic sank on its maiden voyage in 1912, and it was one of the deadliest peacetime maritime disasters in history.
Can a person learn history by playing video games?	Yes, a person can learn history by playing video games, and it is a fun and engaging way to learn about different time periods and events.
Is it true that the Magna Carta was signed in 1215?	Yes, the Magna Carta was signed in 1215 in England, and it is considered a cornerstone of modern democracy and human rights.
Can a person visit ancient pyramids in Egypt?	Yes, a person can visit ancient pyramids in Egypt, and it is a popular tourist attraction that attracts millions of visitors each year.
Is it true that the Berlin Wall fell in 1989?	Yes, the Berlin Wall fell in 1989, marking the end of the Cold War and the reunification of Germany.
Can a person study history without leaving their home?	Yes, a person can study history without leaving their home by using online resources such as books, articles, and documentaries.
Is it true that the American Civil War lasted four years?	Yes, the American Civil War lasted from 1861 to 1865, and it was fought between the Union and the Confederacy over issues such as slavery and states' rights.
Can a person visit historical landmarks in different countries?	Yes, a person can visit historical landmarks in different countries, and it is a great way to learn about different cultures and their contributions to history.

199. I can be a reason for laughter or a cause of tears, but I am not a joke. What am I?

200. I can be a symbol of wealth or a mark of poverty, but I am not a bank. What am I?

201. I can be a source of sustenance or a cause of hunger, but I am not a meal. What am I?

202. I can be a force for protection or a reason for vulnerability, but I am not a wall. What am I?

203. I can be a tool for learning or a source of confusion, but I am not a teacher. What am I?

204. I can be a symbol of freedom or a sign of entrapment, but I am not a cage. What am I?

205. I can be a reason for inspiration or a cause of disappointment, but I am not a hero. What am I?

206. I can be a pathway to success or a route to failure, but I am not a ladder. What am I?

207. I can be a source of power or a cause of weakness, but I am not electricity. What am I?

Category: Sports

Question	Answer
Is it true that Michael Jordan was cut from his high school basketball team?	Yes, Michael Jordan was cut from his high school basketball team, but he went on to become one of the greatest basketball players of all time.
Can a person run a marathon without any training?	No, running a marathon requires proper training and preparation, and it can be dangerous to attempt it without any prior experience.
Is it true that the Tour de France is one of the most grueling cycling races in the world?	Yes, the Tour de France is one of the most grueling cycling races in the world, covering over 2,000 miles in 21 days.
Can a person practice martial arts without a partner?	Yes, a person can practice martial arts without a partner by using techniques such as shadowboxing and practicing forms or katas.
Is it true that the first modern Olympic Games were held in Athens, Greece in 1896?	Yes, the first modern Olympic Games were held in Athens, Greece in 1896, and it featured athletes from 14 countries competing in 43 events.
Can a person play soccer without a soccer ball?	No, soccer requires a soccer ball to be played, but there are variations of the game that can be played with different objects such as a tennis ball or even a makeshift ball made out of socks.
Is it true that Serena Williams has won more Grand Slam titles than any other female tennis player?	Yes, Serena Williams has won 23 Grand Slam titles, making her the most successful female tennis player in the Open Era.
Can a person learn how to swim without taking lessons?	Yes, a person can learn how to swim without taking lessons, but it is recommended to take lessons to learn proper technique and ensure safety.
Is it true that the FIFA World Cup is the most watched sporting event in the world?	Yes, the FIFA World Cup is the most watched sporting event in the world, with an estimated 3.5 billion viewers tuning in for the 2018 tournament.
Can a person practice yoga without any equipment?		Yes, a person can practice yoga without any equipment, and it can be done using just a mat or even a towel on a flat surface.

208. I can be a sign of wisdom or a mark of foolishness, but I am not a proverb. What am I?

209. I can be a tool for communication or a source of isolation, but I am not a phone. What am I?

210. I can be a force for change or a reason for stagnation, but I am not a tide. What am I?

211. I can be a source of inspiration or a cause for irritation, but I am not a song. What am I?

212. I can be a symbol of growth or a mark of decay, but I am not a tree. What am I?

213. I can be a reason for unity or a cause of separation, but I am not a war. What am I?

214. I can be a force of illumination or a source of darkness, but I am not the sun. What am I?

215. I can be a pathway to understanding or a route to confusion, but I am not a lecture. What am I?

216. I can be a sign of success or a symbol of failure, but I am not a grade. What am I?

Category: Technology

Question	Answer
Is it true that Steve Jobs co-founded Apple Inc.?	Yes, Steve Jobs co-founded Apple Inc. in 1976, and it went on to become one of the most successful technology companies in the world.
Can a person code a website without any prior experience?	Yes, a person can code a website without any prior experience, but it requires dedication, patience, and a willingness to learn.
Is it true that the first iPhone was released in 2007?	Yes, the first iPhone was released by Apple Inc. in 2007, and it revolutionized the smartphone industry.
Can a person learn to code using online resources?	Yes, a person can learn to code using online resources such as tutorials, videos, and coding bootcamps.
Is it true that Elon Musk founded Tesla Motors?	Yes, Elon Musk co-founded Tesla Motors in 2003, and it is a company that produces electric cars and renewable energy products.
Can a person repair their own computer without any prior experience?	Yes, a person can repair their own computer without any prior experience, but it is recommended to have some basic knowledge and to follow instructions carefully.
Is it true that the first computer mouse was invented in the 1960s?	Yes, the first computer mouse was invented by Douglas Engelbart in the 1960s, and it was used to control the cursor on a graphical user interface.
Can a person build their own computer from scratch?	Yes, a person can build their own computer from scratch, and it allows for customization and upgrading of components.
Is it true that the first video game was created in the 1950s?	Yes, the first video game was created in the 1950s by physicist William Higinbotham, and it was a simple game of tennis played on an oscilloscope.
Can a person learn how to use software programs without any formal training?	Yes, a person can learn how to use software programs without any formal training, but it requires experimentation and practice to master the different features and functions.

217. I can be a reason for happiness or a cause of sadness, but I am not a movie. What am I?

218. I can be a source of strength or a reason for weakness, but I am not a pill. What am I?

219. I can be a tool for creation or a weapon of destruction, but I am not a hammer. What am I?

220. I can be a force of attraction or a cause of repulsion, but I am not a fragrance. What am I?

221. I can be a sign of life or a symbol of death, but I am not a pulse. What am I?

222. I can be a source of comfort or a reason for discomfort, but I am not a chair. What am I?

223. I can be a reason for peace or a cause of chaos, but I am not a treaty. What am I?

224. I can be a means of escape or a source of entrapment, but I am not a novel. What am I?

225. I can be a symbol of hope or a sign of despair, but I am not a rainbow. What am I?

Category: Unbelievable Facts

Question	Answer
Is it true that a single strand of spaghetti is called a "spaghetto"?	Yes, it is true that a single strand of spaghetti is called a "spaghetto" in Italian.
Can a person survive being struck by lightning multiple times?	It is extremely unlikely, but there have been documented cases of people surviving being struck by lightning multiple times.
Is it true that a sneeze can travel up to 100 miles per hour?	Yes, it is true that a sneeze can travel up to 100 miles per hour, which is why it is important to cover your mouth when sneezing.
Can a person live without a heartbeat?	No, it is not possible for a person to live without a heartbeat, as it is necessary for the circulation of oxygen and nutrients throughout the body.
Is it true that the shortest war in history lasted only 38 minutes?	Yes, the shortest war in history was the Anglo-Zanzibar War in 1896, which lasted only 38 minutes.
Can a person survive without sleep for weeks?	No, it is not possible for a person to survive without sleep for weeks, as sleep is necessary for the body to rest and repair.
Is it true that there is a species of jellyfish that is considered immortal?	Yes, the Turritopsis dohrnii jellyfish is considered immortal because it can revert back to its juvenile form after reaching maturity.
Can a person survive in space without a spacesuit?	No, it is not possible for a person to survive in space without a spacesuit, as the vacuum of space can cause rapid decompression and other serious health issues.
Is it true that a group of flamingos is called a "flamboyance"?	Yes, a group of flamingos is called a "flamboyance" due to their bright colors and showy displays.
Can a person survive being swallowed by a whale?	It is highly unlikely, but there have been rare cases of people surviving being swallowed by a whale and later rescued.

226. I can be a force for protection or a cause of destruction, but I am not a shield. What am I?

227. I can be a tool for learning or a source of ignorance, but I am not a textbook. What am I?

228. I can be a reason for joy or a cause of sorrow, but I am not a gift. What am I?

229. I can be a source of warmth or a reason for coldness, but I am not a heater. What am I?

230. I can be a symbol of love or a mark of hatred, but I am not a heart. What am I?

231. I can be a pathway to success or a route to failure, but I am not a plan. What am I?

232. I can be a reason for laughter or a cause of tears, but I am not a comedian. What am I?

233. I can be a force of change or a source of resistance, but I am not a law. What am I?

234. I can be a sign of growth or a symbol of decline, but I am not a stock. What am I?

Category: Food

Question	Answer
Is it true that chocolate was once used as currency in ancient Mexico?	Yes, chocolate was once used as currency by the Aztecs and Mayans in ancient Mexico.
Can a person develop a food allergy later in life?	Yes, a person can develop a food allergy later in life, even if they have previously eaten the food without any issues.
Is it true that the world's largest pizza was over 130 feet in diameter?	Yes, the world's largest pizza was over 130 feet in diameter and was made in Italy in 2012.
Can a person taste different flavors with different parts of their tongue?	No, the concept of "tongue mapping" is a myth, and taste buds are distributed evenly throughout the tongue.
Is it true that ketchup was once used as medicine?	Yes, ketchup was once used as medicine in the 1800s and was believed to cure ailments such as diarrhea and indigestion.
Can a person eat too much watermelon?	Yes, eating too much watermelon can lead to digestive issues such as diarrhea and stomach cramps due to its high water content.
Is it true that hot sauce can improve digestion?	Yes, hot sauce can improve digestion by increasing the production of stomach acid and enzymes.
Can a person be allergic to a specific type of fruit?	Yes, a person can be allergic to a specific type of fruit, and it is known as oral allergy syndrome.
Is it true that popcorn was once banned from movie theaters?	Yes, popcorn was once banned from movie theaters in the early 1900s because theater owners believed it was too noisy and messy.
Can a person survive solely on a diet of insects?	Yes, a person can survive solely on a diet of insects, as they are a rich source of protein and other nutrients.

235. I can be a reason for excitement or a cause of boredom, but I am not a game. What am I?

236. I can be a source of inspiration or a reason for despair, but I am not a painting. What am I?

237. I can be a tool for expression or a cause of repression, but I am not a speech. What am I?

238. I can be a force for good or a source of evil, but I am not a superhero. What am I?

239. I can be a symbol of wealth or a sign of poverty, but I am not a mansion. What am I?

240. I can be a reason for hope or a cause of disappointment, but I am not a lottery ticket. What am I?

241. I can be a source of stability or a force of instability, but I am not an anchor. What am I?

242. I can be a sign of wisdom or a mark of folly, but I am not a diploma. What am I?

243. I can be a tool for healing or a cause of pain, but I am not a doctor. What am I?

Category: Sports

Question	Answer
Is it true that a tennis ball can reach speeds of up to 163 miles per hour?	Yes, it is true that a tennis ball can reach speeds of up to 163 miles per hour, and it is the fastest recorded serve in tennis history.
Can a person score a goal in soccer by using their head?	Yes, a person can score a goal in soccer by using their head, and it is known as a "header."
Is it true that Michael Jordan was once cut from his high school basketball team?	Yes, Michael Jordan was once cut from his high school basketball team, but he used it as motivation to work harder and become one of the greatest basketball players of all time.
Can a person play basketball while blindfolded?	While it is possible, it is not recommended for safety reasons, and it would be extremely difficult to play basketball while blindfolded.
Is it true that Usain Bolt holds the world record for the fastest 100-meter sprint?	Yes, Usain Bolt holds the world record for the fastest 100-meter sprint, with a time of 9.58 seconds.
Can a person score a touchdown in American football by running with the ball?	Yes, a person can score a touchdown in American football by running with the ball and crossing the opponent's goal line.
Is it true that the Stanley Cup has been used as a cereal bowl?	Yes, the Stanley Cup has been used as a cereal bowl by players and fans alike, and it is considered a tradition in the sport of hockey.
Can a person do a backflip while snowboarding?	Yes, a person can do a backflip while snowboarding, and it is known as a "backside rodeo."
Is it true that Muhammad Ali once fought a Japanese professional wrestler?	Yes, Muhammad Ali once fought a Japanese professional wrestler named Antonio Inoki in a unique hybrid match that was controversial at the time.
Can a person play golf with only one club?	Yes, a person can play golf with only one club, and it is known as "one-club golf."

244. I can be a reason for celebration or a source of frustration, but I am not a party. What am I?

245. I can be a symbol of power or a sign of weakness, but I am not a throne. What am I?

246. I can be a force for growth or a cause of stagnation, but I am not a river. What am I?

247. I can be a pathway to knowledge or a route to confusion, but I am not a library. What am I?

248. I can be a reason for fear or a source of courage, but I am not a nightmare. What am I?

249. I can be a sign of trust or a symbol of betrayal, but I am not a handshake. What am I?

250. I can be a force for connection or a source of division, but I am not a road. What am I?

251. I can be a reason for calmness or a cause of stress, but I am not a vacation. What am I?

252. I can be a source of clarity or a reason for confusion, but I am not a lens. What am I?

Category: Science

Question	Answer
Is it true that the human body contains enough fat to make seven bars of soap?	Yes, it is true that the human body contains enough fat to make seven bars of soap, although it is not recommended or ethical to do so.
Can a person levitate with the power of their mind?	No, levitation with the power of the mind is a fictional concept and is not scientifically possible.
Is it true that the universe is expanding at an accelerating rate?	Yes, the universe is expanding at an accelerating rate, and it is one of the most significant discoveries in modern cosmology.
Can a person create a perpetual motion machine?	No, a perpetual motion machine is a theoretical concept that violates the laws of thermodynamics and is not possible to create.
Is it true that the brain can generate enough electricity to power a light bulb?	Yes, the brain can generate enough electricity to power a small light bulb, but it is a minuscle amount of energy compared to the energy required to power the brain itself
Can a person become invisible with the help of technology?	While there are technologies that can make objects appear invisible, it is not possible for a person to become completely invisible due to the way light interacts with the human body.
Is it true that a cockroach can live for several weeks without its head?	Yes, it is true that a cockroach can live for several weeks without its head because they have a decentralized nervous system and can breathe through small holes in their body.
Can a person survive exposure to outer space without a spacesuit?	No, it is not possible for a person to survive exposure to outer space without a spacesuit due to the lack of oxygen, extreme temperatures, and radiation.
Is it true that the Earth's magnetic field is slowly reversing?	Yes, the Earth's magnetic field is slowly reversing, and it has been happening for millions of years.
Can a person travel faster than the speed of light?	No, it is not possible for a person to travel faster than the speed of light according to the laws of physics.

253. I can be a symbol of endurance or a sign of collapse, but I am not a marathon. What am I?

254. I can be a tool for discovery or a source of ignorance, but I am not a telescope. What am I?

255. I can be a force for transformation or a cause of stagnation, but I am not a chrysalis. What am I?

256. I can be a reason for harmony or a source of discord, but I am not a musical note. What am I?

257. I can be a sign of beauty or a symbol of ugliness, but I am not a sculpture. What am I?

258. I can be a force for awakening or a source of slumber, but I am not an alarm clock. What am I?

259. I can be a reason for connection or a cause of isolation, but I am not a conversation. What am I?

260. I can be a source of nourishment or a reason for hunger, but I am not a farm. What am I?

261. I can be a sign of safety or a symbol of danger, but I am not a seatbelt. What am I?

Category: History

Question	Answer
Is it true that Cleopatra was not actually Egyptian?	Yes, it is true that Cleopatra was not actually Egyptian, but was of Greek descent.
Can a person visit the ruins of the ancient city of Pompeii?	Yes, a person can visit the ruins of the ancient city of Pompeii, which was destroyed by the eruption of Mount Vesuvius in 79 AD.
Is it true that the Great Wall of China is visible from space?	No, it is not true that the Great Wall of China is visible from space with the naked eye, but it can be seen with the help of telescopes and other technology.
Can a person visit the site of the Chernobyl disaster?	Yes, a person can visit the site of the Chernobyl disaster in Ukraine, but it is important to follow safety precautions due to the ongoing radiation risk.
Is it true that the United States once had a president who served two non-consecutive terms?	Yes, Grover Cleveland was the only U.S. president to serve two non-consecutive terms, with a four-year gap between them.
Can a person visit the ancient city of Petra in Jordan?	Yes, a person can visit the ancient city of Petra in Jordan, which is a UNESCO World Heritage Site and one of the most famous archaeological sites in the world.
Is it true that the first Olympic Games were held in ancient Greece?	Yes, the first Olympic Games were held in ancient Greece in 776 BC and were held every four years to honor the god Zeus.
Can a person visit the Palace of Versailles in France?	Yes, a person can visit the Palace of Versailles in France, which was the royal residence of the French monarchs from 1682 until the French Revolution.
Is it true that the Titanic sank on its maiden voyage?	Yes, the Titanic sank on its maiden voyage in 1912 after colliding with an iceberg in the North Atlantic Ocean.
Can a person visit the ruins of Machu Picchu in Peru?	Yes, a person can visit the ruins of Machu Picchu in Peru, which is a UNESCO World Heritage Site and one of the most popular tourist attractions in South America.

262. I can be a force for unity or a cause of division, but I am not a political party. What am I?

263. I can be a reason for relaxation or a source of tension, but I am not a massage. What am I?

264. I can be a symbol of truth or a sign of deception, but I am not a lie detector. What am I?

265. I can be a force for creation or a source of destruction, but I am not a tornado. What am I?

266. I can be a pathway to enlightenment or a route to ignorance, but I am not a guru. What am I?

267. I can be a reason for love or a cause of hatred, but I am not a relationship. What am I?

268. I can be a source of joy or a reason for sorrow, but I am not a wedding. What am I

269. I can be a force for motivation or a cause of procrastination, but I am not a deadline. What am I?

270. I can be a sign of wisdom or a symbol of foolishness, but I am not a pair of glasses. What am I?

Category: Nature

| --- | --- |
Is it true that the largest living organism in the world is a fungus?	Yes, the largest living organism in the world is a fungus known as Armillaria ostoyae, which covers an area of over 2,200 acres in Oregon, USA.
Can a person outrun a cheetah?	No, a person cannot outrun a cheetah, as they are the fastest land animal and can reach speeds of up to 75 miles per hour.
Is it true that a hummingbird's heart beats over 1,000 times per minute?	Yes, it is true that a hummingbird's heart beats over 1,000 times per minute, which is necessary to sustain their high metabolism and rapid wing beats.
Can a person survive a lightning strike?	Yes, a person can survive a lightning strike, but it can cause serious injuries and health issues such as heart damage and neurological problems.
Is it true that the Venus flytrap is native to the United States?	Yes, the Venus flytrap is native to the southeastern United States and is known for its ability to capture and digest insects.
Can a person survive a snake bite without medical treatment?	It depends on the species of snake and the severity of the bite, but it is not recommended to try to survive a snake bite without medical treatment, as it can be fatal.
Is it true that a group of jellyfish is called a "smack"?	Yes, a group of jellyfish is called a "smack" due to the sound they make when they wash up on shore.
Can a person survive falling from a great height with the help of a parachute?	Yes, a person can survive falling from a great height with the help of a parachute, which slows down the descent and reduces the impact of the fall.
Is it true that there is a species of shrimp that can break glass with its claws?	Yes, there is a species of shrimp known as the mantis shrimp that can break glass with its powerful claws, which can strike at speeds of over 50 miles per hour.
Can a person survive a shark attack?	It depends on the severity of the attack and the species of shark, but it is possible for a person to survive a shark attack with prompt medical attention.

271. I can be a reason for celebration or a source of grief, but I am not a birthday. What am I?

272. I can be a tool for expression or a means of repression, but I am not a paintbrush. What am I?

273. I can be a force for adventure or a source of fear, but I am not a roller coaster. What am I?

274. I can be a symbol of opportunity or a sign of limitation, but I am not a door. What am I?

275. I can be a reason for unity or a cause of division, but I am not a sports team. What am I?

276. I can be a source of inspiration or a reason for despair, but I am not a sunrise. What am I?

277. I can be a force for change or a source of stagnation, but I am not a revolution. What am I?

278. I can be a sign of hope or a symbol of dread, but I am not a weather forecast. What am I?

279. I can be a reason for connection or a cause of alienation, but I am not a bridge. What am I?

Category: Technology

Question	Answer
Is it true that the first computer was the size of a room?	Yes, the first computer was the size of a room and was called the Electronic Numerical Integrator and Computer (ENIAC), which was developed in the 1940s.
Can a person use a smartphone as a remote control for their TV?	Yes, a person can use a smartphone as a remote control for their TV with the help of apps such as Apple TV or Google Chromecast.
Is it true that the first video game was created in 1958?	Yes, the first video game was created in 1958 by physicist William Higinbotham and was called "Tennis for Two."
Can a person control a computer with their thoughts?	While it is possible to control some aspects of a computer with brain-computer interfaces (BCIs), it is still in the experimental stage and not widely available.
Is it true that the first cell phone weighed over two pounds?	Yes, the first cell phone weighed over two pounds and was called the Motorola DynaTAC, which was introduced in 1983.
Can a person print 3D objects at home with a 3D printer?	Yes, a person can print 3D objects at home with a 3D printer, which uses digital designs to create physical objects layer by layer.
Is it true that robots have been used in surgery for decades?	Yes, robots have been used in surgery for decades, and they are known as surgical robots or robot-assisted surgery.
Can a person use a virtual reality headset to experience a simulated environment?	Yes, a person can use a virtual reality headset to experience a simulated environment, which can range from gaming to educational and training applications.
Is it true that the first email was sent in the 1970s?	Yes, the first email was sent in the 1970s by computer engineer Ray Tomlinson, who is credited with inventing the use of the "@" symbol in email addresses.
Can a person control their home appliances with a smart speaker?	Yes, a person can control their home appliances with a smart speaker such as Amazon Echo or Google Home, which use voice commands to activate devices such as lights, thermostats, and TVs.

280. I can be a source of creativity or a force of destruction, but I am not a computer. What am I?

281. I can be a symbol of progress or a sign of regression, but I am not a clock. What am I?

282. I can be a pathway to success or a route to failure, but I am not a career. What am I?

283. I can be a reason for laughter or a cause of tears, but I am not a sitcom. What am I?

284. I can be a force for good or a source of evil, but I am not a potion. What am I?

285. I can be a sign of intelligence or a symbol of ignorance, but I am not a brain. What am I?

286. I can be a reason for comfort or a cause of discomfort, but I am not a blanket. What am I?

287. I can be a source of warmth or a reason for coldness, but I am not a fireplace. What am I?

288. I can be a symbol of life or a sign of death, but I am not a flower. What am I?

Category: Food and Drink

Question	Answer
Is it true that carrots were originally purple?	Yes, carrots were originally purple, and it wasn't until the 16th century that Dutch farmers developed orange carrots as a tribute to the House of Orange.
Can a person drink a cocktail that contains a human toe?	Yes, a person can drink a cocktail that contains a human toe, which is a tradition at the Sourdough Saloon in Dawson City, Canada.
Is it true that some cheeses contain live maggots?	Yes, some cheeses such as casu marzu from Sardinia, Italy, contain live maggots that are intentionally added to the cheese during the fermentation process.
Can a person eat a fruit that tastes like chocolate pudding?	Yes, a person can eat a fruit called black sapote, which is also known as the "chocolate pudding fruit" due to its sweet and creamy texture.
Is it true that coffee beans are actually seeds?	Yes, coffee beans are actually seeds that are found inside the fruit of the coffee plant.
Can a person eat a chili pepper that is over 2 million Scoville units?	While it is possible to eat a chili pepper that is over 2 million Scoville units, it is extremely hot and can cause intense pain and health issues.
Is it true that some alcoholic beverages are made with animal parts?	Yes, some alcoholic beverages such as snake wine from Vietnam and Korea and the Icelandic spirit Brennivín are made with animal parts such as snakes, worms, or sheep heads.
Can a person eat a plant that is known as the "meat of the future"?	Yes, a person can eat a plant called jackfruit, which is known as the "meat of the future" due to its meaty texture and versatility in vegetarian and vegan dishes.
Is it true that some people are allergic to water?	Yes, some people are allergic to water, which is a rare condition known as aquagenic urticaria.
Can a person eat a fruit that smells like rotting flesh?	Yes, a person can eat a fruit called durian, which is known for its pungent odor that has been compared to rotting flesh or garbage.

289. I can be a force for encouragement or a source of discouragement, but I am not an award. What am I?

290. I can be a reason for serenity or a cause of turmoil, but I am not a storm. What am I?

291. I can be a symbol of freedom or a sign of confinement, but I am not a cage. What am I?

292. I can be a pathway to discovery or a route to confusion, but I am not a labyrinth. What am I?

293. I can be a reason for security or a cause of vulnerability, but I am not a lock. What am I?

294. I can be a source of happiness or a force of sadness, but I am not a song. What am I?

295. I can be a sign of abundance or a symbol of scarcity, but I am not a harvest. What am I?

296. I can be a force for clarity or a source of obscurity, but I am not a lightbulb. What am I?

297. I can be a reason for harmony or a cause of discord, but I am not an orchestra. What am I?

Category: Sports

Question	Answer
Is it true that the first Olympic marathon was run without shoes?	Yes, the first Olympic marathon was run without shoes by Greek athlete Spyridon Louis in the 1896 Athens Olympics.
Can a person ski on a sand dune?	Yes, a person can ski on a sand dune with the help of specialized sandboards or skis, which are designed to glide on sand.
Is it true that the first World Cup soccer tournament was held in 1930?	Yes, the first World Cup soccer tournament was held in 1930 in Uruguay and was won by the host nation.
Can a person play golf on a glacier?	Yes, a person can play golf on a glacier with the help of specialized equipment such as golf balls with colored inserts and ski boots with spikes.
Is it true that chess is considered a sport?	Yes, chess is considered a sport by the International Olympic Committee and has been recognized as such since 1999.
Can a person play basketball on a trampoline?	Yes, a person can play basketball on a trampoline with the help of specialized trampolines and hoops that are designed for this purpose.
Is it true that the first modern Olympic Games were held in Greece in 1896?	Yes, the first modern Olympic Games were held in Athens, Greece, in 1896 after a hiatus of over 1,500 years.
Can a person surf on a standing wave?	Yes, a person can surf on a standing wave with the help of specialized river surfboards and locations with stationary waves such as Munich's Eisbach river.
Is it true that the first Super Bowl was played in 1967?	Yes, the first Super Bowl was played in 1967 between the Green Bay Packers and the Kansas City Chiefs.
Can a person play soccer on a rooftop?	Yes, a person can play soccer on a rooftop with the help of specially designed mini-pitches that can be installed on top of buildings.

298. I can be a pathway to health or a route to sickness, but I am not a medicine. What am I?

299. I can be a symbol of hope or a sign of despair, but I am not a shooting star. What am I?

300. I can be a force for love or a source of hatred, but I am not a cupid. What am I?

301. I can be a reason for courage or a cause of fear, but I am not a ghost. What am I?

302. I can be a symbol of strength or a sign of weakness, but I am not a mountain. What am I?

303. I can be a pathway to wisdom or a route to foolishness, but I am not a riddle. What am I?

304. I can be a force for connection or a source of isolation, but I am not a telephone. What am I?

305. I can be a reason for peace or a cause of war, but I am not a treaty. What am I?

306. I can be a symbol of prosperity or a sign of poverty, but I am not a bank. What am I?

Category: Space

Question	Answer
Is it true that the planet Jupiter has more moons than any other planet?	Yes, the planet Jupiter has more than 79 known moons, which is the most of any planet in our solar system.
Can a person see the International Space Station from Earth?	Yes, a person can see the International Space Station from Earth with the naked eye as it orbits around the planet at an altitude of about 250 miles.
Is it true that the Moon is moving away from the Earth?	Yes, the Moon is moving away from the Earth at a rate of about 1.5 inches per year due to the effects of tidal friction.
Can a person visit the Hubble Space Telescope?	No, a person cannot visit the Hubble Space Telescope, as it is in orbit around the Earth at an altitude of about 350 miles and is only accessible by astronauts during space missions.
Is it true that the Sun is actually a star?	Yes, the Sun is actually a star and is classified as a G-type main-sequence star, which is also known as a yellow dwarf.
Can a person survive a trip to Mars?	It is currently not possible for a person to survive a trip to Mars with current technology, as the journey would take several months and would expose astronauts to high levels of radiation and other health risks.
Is it true that the Milky Way galaxy is a spiral galaxy?	Yes, the Milky Way galaxy is a spiral galaxy that contains billions of stars, planets, and other celestial objects.

307. I can be a force for growth or a source of decay, but I am not a fertilizer. What am I?

308. I can be a reason for excitement or a cause of boredom, but I am not a roller coaster. What am I?

309. I can be a pathway to happiness or a route to sadness, but I am not a memory. What am I?

310. I can be a symbol of beauty or a sign of ugliness, but I am not a painting. What am I?

311. I am a source of creativity and originality, and I can be found in every person. What am I?

312. I can be cracked or scrambled, but I am not an egg. What am I?

313. I can be hot or cold, but I am not a shower. What am I?

314. I come in different shapes and sizes, and I am filled with knowledge. What am I?

315. I can be used to write, but I am not a pen. What am I?

Category: Space

Question	Answer
Can a person see a shooting star?	Yes, a person can see a shooting star or a meteoroid that burns up upon entering the Earth's atmosphere, creating a streak of light across the sky.
Is it true that there is a planet made entirely of diamonds?	While there is no confirmed planet made entirely of diamonds, some exoplanets have been found to contain large amounts of carbon, which could potentially form diamonds under extreme pressure and heat.
Can a person live on a space station?	Yes, a person can live on a space station such as the International Space Station for extended periods of time, but it requires specialized training and equipment to survive in microgravity and other harsh conditions.
Is it true that there is a black hole at the center of our galaxy?	Yes, there is a supermassive black hole at the center of our galaxy, which is called Sagittarius A* and has a mass of about 4 million times that of the Sun.
Can a person see the Northern Lights from space?	Yes, astronauts aboard the International Space Station can see the Northern Lights or Aurora Borealis from space, which is caused by the interaction of charged particles from the Sun with the Earth's magnetic field.
Is it true that there are planets outside our solar system?	Yes, there are thousands of planets that have been discovered outside our solar system, which are called exoplanets and vary in size, composition, and distance from their host stars.
Can a person jump higher on the Moon than on Earth?	Yes, a person can jump higher on the Moon than on Earth due to the lower gravity, which is about one-sixth of Earth's gravity.
Is it true that there is a theory that our universe is a simulation?	Yes, there is a theory called the simulation hypothesis that suggests that our universe could be a computer simulation created by a more advanced civilization.
Can a person hear sound in space?	No, a person cannot hear sound in space, as sound requires a medium such as air or water to travel, which does not exist in the vacuum of space.
Is it true that the first person to walk on the Moon was Neil Armstrong?	Yes, Neil Armstrong was the first person to walk on the Moon during the Apollo 11 mission in 1969.

316. I have teeth but can't chew, and I am not an animal. What am I?

317. I can be electric or acoustic, but I am not a guitar. What am I?

318. I can be bright or dim, but I am not a star. What am I?

319. I can be found in a gym, but I am not an athlete. What am I?

320. I can be created, copied, and even shared, but I am not a document. What am I?

321. I am part of a tree, but I am not a branch. What am I?

322. I can be found underground, but I am not a worm. What am I?

323. I can help you see, but I am not a pair of glasses. What am I?

324. I can be found in the sky, but I am not a cloud. What am I?

Category: History

Question	Answer
Is it true that the Great Wall of China can be seen from space?	No, the Great Wall of China cannot be seen from space with the naked eye, as it is not visible from low Earth orbit without magnification.
Can a person visit the site where Julius Caesar was assassinated?	Yes, a person can visit the site where Julius Caesar was assassinated in the Roman Forum in Rome, Italy.
Is it true that the United States declared independence from Great Britain in 1776?	Yes, the United States declared independence from Great Britain on July 4, 1776, which is celebrated as Independence Day.
Can a person see the Rosetta Stone in person?	Yes, a person can see the Rosetta Stone in person at the British Museum in London, UK, where it has been on display since 1802.
Is it true that the Taj Mahal was built as a mausoleum for a queen?	Yes, the Taj Mahal was built by Mughal Emperor Shah Jahan as a mausoleum for his beloved wife Mumtaz Mahal, who died in 1631.
Can a person visit the site of the first Olympic Games?	Yes, a person can visit the site of the first Olympic Games in Olympia, Greece, which was held in 776 BCE.
Is it true that the Berlin Wall fell in 1989?	Yes, the Berlin Wall fell in 1989 after nearly three decades of dividing East and West Germany during the Cold War.
Can a person see the Declaration of Independence in person?	Yes, a person can see the Declaration of Independence in person at the National Archives Museum in Washington, D.C., where it is preserved in a special case.
Is it true that the ancient city of Pompeii was destroyed by a volcanic eruption?	Yes, the ancient city of Pompeii was destroyed by the eruption of Mount Vesuvius in 79 CE, which buried the city in ash and preserved it for centuries.
Can a person visit the site of the Battle of Waterloo?	Yes, a person can visit the site of the Battle of Waterloo in Belgium, where Napoleon Bonaparte was defeated by British and allied forces in 1815.

325. I can be carried, but I am not a bag. What am I?

326. I can be used to play, but I am not a toy. What am I?

327. I can be found at the end of a rainbow, but I am not a pot of gold. What am I?

328. I can be sweet or sour, but I am not a candy. What am I?

329. I can be found in a kitchen, but I am not a chef. What am I?

330. I can be found in a castle, but I am not a king. What am I?

331. I can be seen but not touched, and I am not a ghost. What am I?

332. I can be opened or closed, but I am not a door. What am I?

333. I can be drawn but not painted, and I am not a picture. What am I?

Category: Pop Culture

Question	Answer
Is it true that the TV show "Friends" had a reunion special in 2021?	Yes, the TV show "Friends" had a reunion special in 2021, which brought together the original cast for the first time since the show ended in 2004.
Can a person visit the house where Harry Potter was born?	No, the house where Harry Potter was born in the fictional universe is not a real place, as it exists only in J.K. Rowling's books and the subsequent films.
Is it true that the movie "Titanic" won 11 Oscars?	Yes, the movie "Titanic" won 11 Oscars at the 1998 Academy Awards, including Best Picture, Best Director, and Best Original Song.
Can a person attend a live taping of "Saturday Night Live"?	Yes, a person can attend a live taping of "Saturday Night Live" in New York City, but tickets are limited and often require a lottery or standby system.
Is it true that the band "The Beatles" broke up in 1970?	Yes, "The Beatles" officially broke up in 1970 after a decade of making music and achieving worldwide fame.

334. I can be found in a park, but I am not a bench. What am I?

335. I can be found in a classroom, but I am not a student. What am I?

336. I can be found in a theater, but I am not an actor. What am I?

337. I can be found in a garden, but I am not a flower. What am I?

338. I can be found in a toolbox, but I am not a hammer. What am I?

339. I can be found in a museum, but I am not a painting. What am I?

340. I can be found in a forest, but I am not a tree. What am I?

341. I can be found in the sea, but I am not a fish. What am I?

342. I can be found in a desert, but I am not a cactus. What am I?

Category: Pop Culture

Question	Answer
Is it true that the TV show "Stranger Things" is set in the 1980s?	Yes, the TV show "Stranger Things" is set in the 1980s and pays homage to popular culture and trends of that era.
Can a person see the Batmobile in person?	Yes, a person can see the Batmobile in person at various locations such as car shows, museums, and theme parks.
Is it true that the "Star Wars" franchise has a dedicated holiday?	Yes, the "Star Wars" franchise has a dedicated holiday called "May the Fourth" or "Star Wars Day," which is celebrated on May 4th every year.
Can a person attend a live taping of "The Ellen Show"?	Yes, a person can attend a live taping of "The Ellen Show" in Burbank, California, but tickets are limited and often require a lottery or standby system.
Is it true that the TV show "The Simpsons" has been on the air for over 30 years?	Yes, the TV show "The Simpsons" has been on the air for over 30 years, making it one of the longest-running primetime TV shows in history.
Can a person visit the real-life location of "Breaking Bad"?	Yes, a person can visit various real-life locations featured in the TV show "Breaking Bad" in Albuquerque, New Mexico, such as the car wash and the candy store.
Is it true that the movie "Jaws" was based on a book?	Yes, the movie "Jaws" was based on a novel by Peter Benchley, which tells the story of a man-eating great white shark terrorizing a beach town.
Can a person attend a live performance by Beyoncé?	Yes, a person can attend a live performance by Beyoncé during her concert tours, which feature elaborate stage productions and choreography.
Is it true that the TV show "Game of Thrones" is based on a book series?	Yes, the TV show "Game of Thrones" is based on a book series called "A Song of Ice and Fire" by George R. R. Martin.

343. I can be found on a farm, but I am not a tractor. What am I?

344. I can be found in a zoo, but I am not a lion. What am I?

345. I can be found in the sky, but I am not an airplane. What am I?

346. I can be found on a beach, but I am not a seashell. What am I?

347. I am a protector of the night, yet I am silent and unseen. What am I?

348. I have many legs, but I don't walk. People use me to reach high places. What am I?

349. I start big and end small, and I am present every day. What am I?

350. I can hold many things, but I never complain. What am I?

351. I am a home that's always moving, carrying precious cargo. What am I?

Category: Animals

Question	Answer
Is it true that a group of flamingos is called a flamboyance?	Yes, a group of flamingos is called a flamboyance, and can contain hundreds or even thousands of birds.
Can a person own a pet hedgehog?	It depends on the laws and regulations of the person's country or state, as some jurisdictions prohibit the ownership of hedgehogs as pets.
Is it true that some animals can regenerate body parts?	Yes, some animals such as salamanders and starfish have the ability to regenerate body parts such as limbs and organs, which is a rare and remarkable adaptation.
Can a person see a blue lobster?	Yes, a person can see a blue lobster, which is a rare genetic mutation that causes the lobster's shell to turn blue instead of the typical brownish-green color.
Is it true that a group of pugs is called a grumble?	Yes, a group of pugs is called a grumble, which is a fitting name for these lovable and sometimes vocal dogs.
Can a person see a giant squid in the wild?	It is rare to see a giant squid in the wild, as they typically live in the deep sea and are elusive and difficult to study.
Is it true that elephants can communicate with each other using infrasound?	Yes, elephants can communicate with each other using infrasound, which is a type of low-frequency sound that is below the range of human hearing.
Can a person have a pet chameleon?	Yes, a person can have a pet chameleon, but it requires specialized care and a suitable environment to meet their unique needs.	Is it true that dolphins have names for each other?	While it is not yet fully understood, some studies suggest that dolphins have unique vocalizations or "signature whistles" that may function as names for individual dolphins.

352. I am full of holes, yet I am still able to hold water. What am I?

353. I am sometimes sweet, sometimes bitter, and can be found in many different colors. What am I?

354. I come in many shapes and sizes, but you'll always find me in the sky. What am I?

355. I can be tough or tender, and I come in a variety of colors. What am I?

356. I am a part of a meal, but I am not food. What am I?

357. I am a word of letters three, add two and fewer there will be. What am I?

358. I am everywhere, but you cannot see me. Yet, when I'm gone, you'll know. What am I?

359. I bring light to dark spaces, but I disappear when you turn your head. What am I?

360. I can be loud or quiet, and I am always changing. What am I?

Category: Animals

Question	Answer
Can a person see a giant tortoise in the wild?	Yes, a person can see a giant tortoise in the wild on islands such as the Galapagos Islands and Aldabra Atoll, where they are native and protected.
Is it true that sloths only defecate once a week?	Yes, sloths have a very slow metabolism and only defecate once a week, which is an adaptation that helps them conserve energy and avoid detection by predators.
Can a person see a white tiger in the wild?	No, a person cannot see a white tiger in the wild, as they are a rare genetic variation of the Bengal tiger and are mostly found in zoos and wildlife sanctuaries.
Is it true that honeybees can recognize human faces?	Yes, honeybees have been shown to have the ability to recognize human faces and differentiate between them using visual cues such as facial features and clothing.
Can a person keep a pet penguin?	No, it is illegal and unethical to keep a pet penguin, as they are wild animals that require specific environmental and social conditions to thrive.
Is it true that kangaroos can jump up to three times their own body length?	Yes, kangaroos have powerful hind legs that allow them to jump up to three times their own body length, which is an adaptation that helps them navigate their environment and evade predators.

361. I am fragile, but I can also make things stronger. What am I?

362. I am used by many, but I can still be a mystery. What am I?

363. I am a type of fuel, but you cannot burn me. What am I?

364. I have many teeth, but I cannot eat. What am I?

365. I have many keys, but I cannot open a door. What am I?

366. I am made of wood, but I cannot float. What am I?

367. I have a spine, but I am not an animal. What am I?

368. I am always in front of you, but you can never touch me. What am I?

369. I am a traveler, but I have no legs. What am I?

Category: Technology

Question	Answer
Is it true that self-driving cars exist?	Yes, self-driving cars or autonomous vehicles are being developed and tested by various companies and have the potential to revolutionize transportation and reduce accidents caused by human error.
Can a person print a 3D object at home?	Yes, a person can print a 3D object at home with a 3D printer, which uses digital designs to create physical objects layer by layer using various materials such as plastics and metals.
Is it true that the first computer virus was created in 1983?	Yes, the first computer virus called "Elk Cloner" was created by a high school student named Rich Skrenta in 1983 and infected Apple II computers.
Can a person control their home appliances with their phone?	Yes, a person can control their home appliances with their phone using smart home technology such as Wi-Fi-enabled plugs and switches, which allow remote control and automation of devices.
Is it true that the first website was created in 1991?	Yes, the first website was created by British computer scientist Tim Berners-Lee in 1991 and provided information about the World Wide Web project.
Can a person use a virtual reality headset to play games?	Yes, a person can use a virtual reality headset to play games and experience immersive and interactive virtual environments that simulate real-world experiences.
Is it true that the first email was sent in 1971?	Yes, the first email was sent by computer engineer Ray Tomlinson in 1971, which was a test message sent between two computers connected to the ARPANET network.
Can a person use a drone to take aerial photos and videos?	Yes, a person can use a drone equipped with a camera to take aerial photos and videos, which is a popular hobby and professional tool for photography and videography.
Is it true that the first text message was sent in 1992?	Yes, the first text message was sent by British engineer Neil Papworth in 1992, which was a "Merry Christmas" message sent from a computer to a mobile phone.
Is it true that the first computer mouse was invented in 1963?	Yes, the first computer mouse was invented by computer scientist Douglas Engelbart in 1963 and used a wooden shell and two wheels to control the cursor on a computer screen.

370. I can be cracked, made, told, and played. What am I?

371. I have a head and a tail, but no body. What am I?

372. I am full of letters, but I have no words. What am I?

373. I am always hungry and must be fed, but if I drink water, I'll die. What am I?

374. I am not alive, but I can grow. I don't have lungs, but I need air. What am I?

375. I am a word, but I am not in the dictionary. What am I?

376. I can be black, white, or both. I am a part of many games. What am I?

377. I am found in the water but am never wet. What am I?

378. I have a neck but no head. What am I?

Category: Technology

Question	Answer
Is it true that the first iPhone was released in 2007?	Yes, the first iPhone was released by Apple in 2007 and revolutionized the mobile phone industry with its touch screen interface and advanced features.
Can a person control their TV with their voice?	Yes, a person can control their TV with their voice using smart assistants such as Amazon Alexa and Google Assistant, which are integrated into some TV models.
Is it true that self-driving cars exist?	Yes, self-driving cars or autonomous vehicles are being developed and tested by various companies and have the potential to revolutionize transportation and reduce accidents caused by human error.
Can a person print a 3D object at home?	Yes, a person can print a 3D object at home with a 3D printer, which uses digital designs to create physical objects layer by layer using various materials such as plastics and metals.
Is it true that the first computer virus was created in 1983?	Yes, the first computer virus called "Elk Cloner" was created by a high school student named Rich Skrenta in 1983 and infected Apple II computers.
Can a person control their home appliances with their phone?	Yes, a person can control their home appliances with their phone using smart home technology such as Wi-Fi-enabled plugs and switches, which allow remote control and automation of devices.
Is it true that the first website was created in 1991?	Yes, the first website was created by British computer scientist Tim Berners-Lee in 1991 and provided information about the World Wide Web project.
Is it true that the first mobile phone was invented in 1973?	Yes, the first mobile phone was invented by Motorola engineer Martin Cooper in 1973 and weighed over two pounds and cost thousands of dollars.
Can a person use a tablet to read books and magazines?	Yes, a person can use a tablet to read books and magazines using various e-reader apps and services, which offer a wide selection of digital books and publications.
Is it true that the first video game was created in 1958?	Yes, the first video game called "Tennis for Two" was created by physicist William Higinbotham in 1958 and used an oscilloscope to display a simulated tennis game.

379. I can make things colder, but I am not a freezer. What am I?

380. I am taken from a mine, and shut up in a wooden case, from which I am never released, and yet I am used by almost every person. What am I?

381. I have many needles, but I do not sew. What am I?

382. I am always running, but I never get tired. What am I?

383. I have a face but no eyes, hands but no arms. What am I?

384. I am always in motion, but I never move. What am I?

385. I am essential to life but can also be deadly. What am I?

386. I can be lost or found, but I cannot be touched. What am I?

387. I can be shared by many or owned by one. What am I?

Category: Science

Question	Answer
Is it true that the Earth's magnetic field protects us from solar radiation?	Yes, the Earth's magnetic field acts as a shield against solar wind and cosmic radiation, which can be harmful to living organisms and electronic devices.
Can a person see a black hole?	No, a person cannot see a black hole directly, as they do not emit light and are invisible to telescopes and other instruments.
Is it true that the Earth's atmosphere is mostly nitrogen and oxygen?	Yes, the Earth's atmosphere is mostly composed of nitrogen (78%) and oxygen (21%), with trace amounts of other gases such as carbon dioxide and argon.
Can a person visit the International Space Station?	While it is not currently open for public visits, a person can potentially visit the International Space Station as part of a commercial spaceflight or government mission in the future.
Is it true that the sun is a star?	Yes, the sun is a star and the closest star to Earth, which powers our planet with energy and light through nuclear fusion reactions.
Can a person see a comet in the sky?	Yes, a person can see a comet in the sky when it passes close enough to Earth and becomes visible with the naked eye or binoculars.
Is it true that the Earth is the only planet with liquid water on its surface?	As far as we know, the Earth is the only planet with liquid water on its surface, which is a crucial component for life as we know it.
Can a person see the Northern Lights?	Yes, a person can see the Northern Lights or Aurora Borealis in areas near the Earth's magnetic poles when charged particles from the sun collide with the Earth's atmosphere and create a colorful light display.

388. I make two people out of one. What am I?

389. I am used to keep things in place, but I am not a lock. What am I?

390. I am a source of entertainment, but I never speak. What am I?

391. I am a type of cover, but I am not a blanket. What am I?

392. I am always coming, but I never arrive. What am I?

393. I can be hot or cold and sometimes cause pain. What am I?

394. I can be found in a pocket, but I am not money. What am I?

395. I have no beginning, middle, or end. What am I?

396. I am a part of you, but I can be stolen. What am I?

Category: Science

Question	Answer
Is it true that the human body contains trillions of cells?	Yes, the human body is composed of trillions of cells, which make up tissues, organs, and systems that enable various functions and processes.
Can a person see a meteor shower?	Yes, a person can see a meteor shower when the Earth passes through a stream of debris left by a comet or asteroid, which creates a bright streak of light in the sky known as a shooting star.
Is it true that the Earth's core is mostly composed of iron and nickel?	Yes, the Earth's core is mostly composed of iron (85%) and nickel (10%), which generate a magnetic field and influence the planet's geology and climate.
Can a person visit a volcano?	Yes, a person can visit various volcanoes around the world that are accessible and safe to visit, but precautions and permits may be necessary depending on the location and activity level of the volcano.
Is it true that the human body contains DNA?	Yes, the human body contains DNA or deoxyribonucleic acid, which is a molecule that carries genetic information and influences various traits and characteristics of living organisms.
Can a person see the rings of Saturn?	Yes, a person can see the rings of Saturn through a telescope or binoculars, which are made up of rock and ice particles and are a distinctive feature of the planet.
Is it true that the Earth's rotation is slowing down?	Yes, the Earth's rotation is slowing down gradually over time, which is caused by various factors such as tidal forces and the redistribution of mass within the planet.

397. I have three eyes but only one leg. What am I?

398. I can be turned on, but I am not a switch. What am I?

399. I can be simple or complex, but I am not a math problem. What am I?

400. I am a type of wave, but I am not in the ocean. What am I?

401. I can be sweet or sour, but I am not candy. What am I?

402. I am found in many shapes, but I am not a geometric figure. What am I?

403. I can be measured, but I cannot be seen. What am I?

404. I am a form of transport, but I do not have wheels. What am I?

405. I am an object that contains knowledge, but I am not a book. What am I?

Category: History

Question	Answer
Is it true that the pyramids of Giza were built over 4,000 years ago?	Yes, the pyramids of Giza in Egypt were built over 4,500 years ago as tombs for pharaohs and their consorts, and are considered some of the most impressive and enduring architectural achievements in human history.
Can a person visit the Great Wall of China?	Yes, a person can visit the Great Wall of China, which spans over 13,000 miles and was built over several centuries as a fortification and symbol of Chinese civilization.
Is it true that the French Revolution occurred in the late 18th century?	Yes, the French Revolution was a period of political and social upheaval that occurred in France from 1789 to 1799, which resulted in the overthrow of the monarchy and the establishment of a republic.
Can a person see the Rosetta Stone in person?	Yes, a person can see the Rosetta Stone in person at the British Museum in London, which is a stone slab inscribed with three scripts that helped decipher ancient Egyptian hieroglyphs.
Is it true that the first Olympic Games were held in ancient Greece?	Yes, the first Olympic Games were held in ancient Greece in 776 BCE and featured various athletic competitions and religious ceremonies that were dedicated to the gods.
Can a person visit the ruins of Pompeii?	Yes, a person can visit the ruins of Pompeii in Italy, which was a Roman city that was buried under ash and pumice after the eruption of Mount Vesuvius in 79 CE and preserved for centuries until rediscovered in the 18th century.
Is it true that the American Civil War occurred in the 19th century?	Yes, the American Civil War was a major conflict that occurred in the United States from 1861 to 1865, which was fought over issues such as slavery, states' rights, and the preservation of the Union.

Are you Ready for the Challenge- What Am I?

406. I am a type of connection, but I am not a bridge. What am I?

407. I can be smooth or rough, but I am not a surface. What am I?

408. I can be fast or slow, but I am not a race. What am I?

409. I can be long or short, but I am not a ruler. What am I?

410. I am a tool for creation, but I am not a paintbrush. What am I?

411. I can be sharp or dull, but I am not a knife. What am I?

412. I can be bright or dim, but I am not a lightbulb. What am I?

413. I can be hard or soft, but I am not a pillow. What am I?

414. I can be heavy or light, but I am not a weight. What am I?

Category: History

Question	Answer
Can a person visit the Colosseum in Rome?	Yes, a person can visit the Colosseum in Rome, which is an iconic amphitheater that was built in the 1st century CE and used for gladiatorial contests, animal hunts, and public spectacles.
Is it true that the Renaissance was a period of cultural and artistic revival in Europe?	Yes, the Renaissance was a period of intellectual and artistic awakening that occurred in Europe from the 14th to the 17th century, which saw the rediscovery and reevaluation of classical texts, as well as advancements in science, technology, and the arts
Can a person visit the Taj Mahal in India?	Yes, a person can visit the Taj Mahal in India, which is a magnificent mausoleum that was built in the 17th century by the Mughal emperor Shah Jahan in memory of his beloved wife Mumtaz Mahal.
Is it true that the Industrial Revolution began in the 18th century?	Yes, the Industrial Revolution was a period of technological and economic growth that began in Britain in the late 18th century and spread to other parts of Europe and the United States, which saw the development of new machines and processes that transformed manufacturing and transportation.
Can a person visit Machu Picchu in Peru?	Yes, a person can visit Machu Picchu in Peru, which is an ancient Incan citadel that was built in the 15th century and rediscovered in 1911 by archaeologist Hiram Bingham.

415. I am a type of language, but I am not spoken. What am I?

416. I can be thick or thin, but I am not a slice of bread. What am I?

417. I can be found in a corner, but I am not a spider. What am I?

418. I can be a sign of victory or a symbol of surrender, but I am not a trophy. What am I?

419. I can be smooth or crunchy, but I am not peanut butter. What am I?

420. I can be open or closed, but I am not a door. What am I?

421. I can be long-lasting or temporary, but I am not a battery. What am I?

422. I am a type of shelter, but I am not a house. What am I?

423. I can be expensive or cheap, but I am not a price tag. What am I?

Category: Food

Question	Answer
Is it true that chocolate was originally consumed as a beverage?	Yes, chocolate was originally consumed as a bitter beverage by the Maya and Aztec civilizations in Central America, and later became popular in Europe as a luxury item.
Can a person eat a durian fruit?	Yes, a person can eat a durian fruit, which is a spiky tropical fruit that is known for its strong odor and custard-like flesh with a sweet and creamy flavor.
Is it true that sushi originated in Japan?	Yes, sushi is a traditional Japanese dish that consists of vinegared rice combined with various toppings such as fish, vegetables, and egg, and is often served with soy sauce and wasabi.
Is it true that potatoes are native to South America?	Yes, potatoes are native to South America and were domesticated by indigenous people over 7,000 years ago, before being introduced to Europe and other parts of the world.
Is it true that tomatoes were once thought to be poisonous?	Yes, tomatoes were once believed to be poisonous and were avoided by many people until the 18th century, when they became more widely accepted as a food item.
Is it true that bananas are berries?	Yes, bananas are technically considered berries because they are derived from a single flower with multiple ovaries and contain seeds, which distinguishes them from other fruits such as strawberries or apples.
Is it true that honey never spoils?	Yes, honey has antimicrobial properties and a low water content, which prevents the growth of bacteria and other organisms that can cause spoilage, and can last indefinitely if stored properly.

424. I am a source of warmth, but I am not a blanket. What am I?

425. I can be found on a desk, but I am not a computer. What am I?

426. I can be worn, but I am not clothing. What am I?

427. I can be a source of power, but I am not a battery. What am I?

428. I am a type of communication, but I am not a letter. What am I?

429. I can be found in the sky, but I am not a cloud. What am I?

430. I can be sweet or spicy, but I am not a dessert. What am I?

431. I can be round or square, but I am not a shape. What am I?

432. I can be wet or dry, but I am not a towel. What am I?

Category: Animals

Question	Answer
Is it true that ostriches can run faster than horses?	Yes, ostriches are the fastest land animals and can run at speeds of up to 43 miles per hour, which is faster than most horses.
Is it true that the giant squid is the largest invertebrate in the world?	Yes, the giant squid is the largest invertebrate in the world and can reach lengths of up to 43 feet, with eyes the size of basketballs and tentacles armed with sharp suckers.
Is it true that chameleons can change color to blend in with their surroundings?	Yes, chameleons have the ability to change color and pattern to camouflage themselves and communicate with other chameleons, which is achieved through specialized cells called chromatophores in their skin.
Is it true that the blue whale is the largest animal on Earth?	Yes, the blue whale is the largest animal on Earth and can grow up to 100 feet in length and weigh over 200 tons, with a heart the size of a car and a tongue that can weigh as much as an elephant.
Is it true that elephants can communicate with infrasonic sounds?	Yes, elephants have the ability to communicate with low-frequency sounds that are below the range of human hearing and can travel long distances through the ground, which helps them to stay in contact with other elephants and detect potential threats.
Is it true that crocodiles can go without food for months?	Yes, crocodiles have the ability to survive for months without food, thanks to their slow metabolism and efficient use of energy, which enables them to store nutrients and wait for the next opportunity to hunt.
Is it true that bats are the only mammals that can fly?	Yes, bats are the only mammals that are capable of sustained flight, thanks to their wings that are made up of thin membranes stretched over elongated fingers, which enable them to navigate and capture prey in the dark.
Is it true that a group of flamingos is called a flamboyance?	Yes, a group of flamingos is indeed called a flamboyance, which is a fitting name for these colorful and graceful birds that are known for their distinctive long legs and curved bills.

433. I am a source of energy, but I am not electricity. What am I?

434. I can be large or small, but I am not a size. What am I?

435. I can be a source of comfort, but I am not a hug. What am I?

436. I can be found in the garden, but I am not a plant. What am I?

437. I can be part of a game, but I am not a player. What am I?

438. I can be found on a ship, but I am not a sailor. What am I?

439. I can be a source of inspiration, but I am not a muse. What am I?

440. I can be used to build, but I am not a hammer. What am I?

441. I can be found on a stage, but I am not an actor. What am I?

442. I can be a source of guidance, but I am not a teacher. What am I?

443. I can be found in the kitchen, but I am not a chef. What am I?

444. I can be a source of joy, but I am not a toy. What am I?

Key To the Riddles

1. Clouds
2. Shadow
3. Smartphone
4. Lenses
5. An address
6. A cemetery
7. A ring
8. An idea
9. A question
10. Struggle
11. A book
12. A feather
13. Silence
14. A candle
15. A digital clock
16. A map
17. A river
18. Time
19. An eye
20. A bridge
21. A star
22. An echo
23. A bed
24. A taste
25. A smile
26. A shadow
27. A fragrance
28. Imagination
29. A reflection
30. A signpost
31. A shadow
32. An onion
33. Time
34. A clock
35. Music
36. A movie
37. A promise
38. A piano
39. A memory of music
40. A tree
41. Photograph
42. A kind act
43. A stone on the ground
44. A trend
45. Knowledge
46. Conversation
47. Stars
48. Fire
49. A story
50. A shadow
51. A forest
52. Glue
53. A secret
54. Art
55. A rainbow
56. A reputation
57. Weather
58. Blanket
59. A rope
60. A scent
61. Pressure
62. Wind
63. A dream
64. Time
65. A fence
66. A drink
67. Music
68. A feeling
69. A mirror
70. A plant
71. A book
72. A position
73. Time
74. Prophecy
75. A calendar
76. Art
77. A gift
78. A memory
79. Rose
80. Water
81. Fear
82. A presence/Photo
83. A diary

84.	Stairs	114.	Communicat ion	146.	Wind
85.	A gesture			147.	Rose
86.	Air	115.	Candle	148.	Gravity
87.	Lighthouse	116.	Pillow	149.	Mistake
88.	A Moment /time	117.	Letter	150.	Fire
		118.	Keys	151.	Question
89.	Light	119.	Wheel	152.	Riddle
90.	The internet	120.	Reflection	153.	Change
91.	A topic	121.	Cane	154.	Balance
92.	A hug	122.	Secret	155.	Voice
93.	A pillow	123.	Handshake	156.	Riddle
94.	The sun	124.	Wind	157.	Sunrise
95.	A symbol	125.	Whisper	158.	Belief
96.	Change	126.	Choice	159.	Choice
97.	Art	127.	Mirror	160.	Oxygen
98.	A shadow	128.	Technology	161.	Clothing
99.	A choice	129.	Thought	162.	Time
100.	A memory	130.	Joke	163.	Experience
101.	A decision	131.	Gesture	164.	Crown
102.	A spark	132.	Choice	165.	Mask
103.	A storm	133.	Exercise	166.	Silence
104.	A secret keeper	134.	Knowledge	167.	Expectation
		135.	Hands	168.	Adventure
105.	A journey	136.	Memory	169.	Signal
106.	A dove	137.	Safe	170.	Ruin
107.	A habit	138.	Memory	171.	Surprise
108.	A city	139.	History	172.	Trust
109.	A lighthouse	140.	Dream	173.	Knowledge
110.	A challenge	141.	Window	174.	Vision
111.	Shadow	142.	Imagination	175.	Star
112.	Flowers	143.	Water	176.	Music
113.	Voice	144.	Scar	177.	Change
		145.	News	178.	Deadline

179.	Decision	212.	Rust	243.	Words
180.	Statue	213.	Belief	244.	Goals
181.	Invention	214.	Knowledge	245.	Leadership
182.	Barrier	215.	Communication	246.	Change
183.	Memory			247.	Questions
184.	Technology	216.	Medal	248.	Fear
185.	Promise	217.	News	249.	Loyalty
186.	Movement	218.	Support	250.	Communication
187.	Taste	219.	Words		
188.	Oxygen	220.	A magnet	251.	Balance
189.	Shadow	221.	Breath	252.	Thoughts
190.	Mountain	222.	Cloth	253.	Perseverance
191.	Imagination	223.	Decision	254.	Curiosity
192.	Touch	224.	Dream	255.	Adaptation
193.	Friendship	225.	Light at the end of tunnel	256.	Cooperation
194.	Power			257.	Perception
195.	Flag	226.	Fire	258.	Dreams
196.	Hug	227.	Internet	259.	Technology
197.	Breath	228.	Memory	260.	Knowledge
198.	Risk	229.	Hug	261.	Warning signs
199.	Story	230.	Gesture		
200.	Home	231.	Choice	262.	Culture
201.	Thirst	232.	Story	263.	Ambiance
202.	Insurance	233.	Mindset	264.	Honesty
203.	Equation	234.	Development	265.	Nature
204.	Chains	235.	Conversation	266.	Education
205.	Role model	236.	Song	267.	Compassion
206.	Crossroad	237.	Art	268.	Emotions
207.	Confidence	238.	Power	269.	Change
208.	Riddle	239.	Money	270.	Humor
209.	Social media	240.	Opportunity	271.	Accomplishments
210.	Momentum	241.	Emotions		
211.	Idea	242.	Decisions	272.	Art

273.	Risk	305.	Ideology	338.	Screwdriver
274.	Possibilities	306.	Economy	339.	Sculpture
275.	Values	307.	Time	340.	Mushroom
276.	Ambition	308.	Imagination	341.	Coral
277.	Progress	309.	Perspective	342.	Sand dune
278.	Uncertainty	310.	Perception	343.	Haystack
279.	Empathy	311.	Imagination	344.	Peacock
280.	Imagination	312.	Code	345.	Kite
281.	Innovation	313.	Coffee	346.	Wave
282.	Choices	314.	Book	347.	Moon
283.	Comedy	315.	Pencil	348.	Ladder
284.	Intentions	316.	Comb	349.	Daylight
285.	Learning	317.	Violin	350.	Bag
286.	Clothing	318.	Light bulb	351.	Car
287.	Affection	319.	Treadmill	352.	Sponge
288.	Time	320.	Idea	353.	Chocolate
289.	Support	321.	Roots	354.	Cloud
290.	Inner peace	322.	Subway	355.	Paper
291.	Choice	323.	Light	356.	Plate
292.	Education	324.	Rainbow	357.	Few
293.	Privacy	325.	Umbrella	358.	Air
294.	Memory	326.	Instrument	359.	Stars
295.	Wealth	327.	Colors	360.	Music
296.	Communication	328.	Lemonade	361.	Glass
		329.	Fridge	362.	Language
297.	Cooperation	330.	Throne	363.	Electricity
298.	Lifestyle	331.	Shadow	364.	Comb
299.	Attitude	332.	Window	365.	Piano
300.	Compassion	333.	Line	366.	Wooden chair
301.	Confidence	334.	Swing		
302.	Resilience	335.	Blackboard	367.	Book
303.	Experience	336.	Curtain	368.	Future
304.	Friendship	337.	Path	369.	Train

370. Joke	396. Identity	421. Friendship
371. Coin	397. Traffic light	422. Tent
372. Alphabet soup	398. Television	423. Gift
	399. Relationship	424. Fireplace
373. Fire	400. Sound wave	425. Pen holder
374. Plant	401. Fruit	426. Watch
375. Misspell	402. Candy	427. Solar panel
376. Chess piece	403. Time	428. Email
377. Reflection	404. Helicopter	429. Satellite
378. Bottle	405. Encyclopedia	430. Salsa
379. Ice		431. Button
380. Pencil	406. Wi-Fi signal	432. Sand
381. Pine tree	407. Voice	433. Sunlight
382. Clock	408. Music tempo	434. Box
383. Clock face	409. Story	435. Pillow
384. Earth	410. Pen	436. Garden gnome
385. Water	411. Wit	
386. Memory	412. Firefly	437. Board game
387. Idea	413. Mattress	438. Anchor
388. Mirror	414. Feather	439. Sunset
389. Paperclip	415. Body language	440. Brick
390. Television		441. Microphone
391. Umbrella	416. Wire	442. Mentor
392. Tomorrow	417. Dust	443. Pot
393. Temperature	418. White flag	444. Laughter
394. Pocket lint	419. Ice cream	
395. Circle	420. Book	

If you like the book, please review us at Amazon

Ignite your Intellect: Books for Smart Kids

Other Books in this series

Skills for Life: The Ultimate Guide for Smart Kids to Succeed!

" This book is designed to help kids between the ages of 8 and 12 develop the essential life skills they need to succeed in the modern world. From managing emotions to communicating effectively, each Chapter provides practical tips and **Example**s to help kids understand the importance of each skill and how to develop it effectively. We believe that these 11 essential life skills will help kids become confident, adaptable, and resilient individuals who are ready to tackle any challenge that comes their way. So, let's get started on this exciting journey of growth and development!

Made in United States
Troutdale, OR
11/29/2024

25468335R00060